**Maureen Little** is a gardener wi... in the commercial cultivation of ... enthusiast and beekeeper. She has ... herb and bee gardening and garden design. She is a member of the Herb Society and contributes to several national gardening and self-sufficiency magazines. Maureen has advised the RHS on herbs and gardening for bees, and offers courses in these areas to both the public and gardening societies. Maureen's most recent books are *The Bee Garden, Plants and Planting Plans for a Bee Garden, The Kitchen Herb Garden* and *The Little Book of Popular Perennials*. She lives in Preston.

## *Also by Maureen Little*

Plants and Planting Plans for a Bee Garden

The Bee Garden

The Kitchen Herb Garden

The Little Book of Popular Perennials

Country Skills and Crafts

# *Home Herbal*

## Maureen Little

Constable & Robinson Ltd
55–56 Russell Square
London WC1B 4HP
www.constablerobinson.com

First published in the UK by How To Books,
an imprint of Constable & Robinson Ltd, 2014

A copy of the British Library Cataloguing in Publication
Data is available from the British Library

ISBN 978-1-84528-542-5 (paperback)
ISBN 978-1-84528-545-6 (ebook)

Printed and bound by
CPI Group (UK) Ltd, Croydon, CR0 4YY

1 3 5 7 9 10 8 6 4 2

*For*
*Ruby and Luke*

# Acknowledgements

Once again I am indebted to my many wonderful relatives, friends and colleagues who provide unceasing encouragement and inspiration. Any mistakes are entirely my own.

Thanks especially to my family – Georg, Becca and James, not forgetting Martin and Katie and the next generation of herb growers (I hope!), Ruby and Luke.

My thanks also go to Giles Lewis and Nikki Read – without them this book, and the ones before it, would never have been written, and I am so grateful to them for their continued support.

# Contents

## CHAPTER 1
## Growing, Harvesting, Preserving and Storing Your Herbs

## CHAPTER 2
## Planting Plans

CHAPTER 3

# Herbs for First-aid and Remedies

CHAPTER 4

# Cosmetic Herbs

# *Contents*

# *Important Notice*

This book contains solely the views and opinions of the author. It is intended to provide interesting, helpful and informative material on the subjects addressed. It is sold with the understanding that it does not contain professional guidance and/or recommendations. The author and publisher disclaim all responsibility for any liability, loss or risk, personal or otherwise, incurred as a consequence, directly or indirectly, of the use and/or application of any of the contents of this book.

All reasonable care has been taken in the compilation of this book. The information it contains, however, is not a guide to self-diagnosis and treatment, and must not be substituted for medical care carried out under professional supervision by a qualified medical practitioner.

Pregnant or lactating women should also seek professional advice before taking or using *any* non-prescription treatments.

Readers are advised to consult a qualified medical practitioner for individual advice.

# Introduction

*How could such sweet and wholesome hours*
*Be reckoned but with herbs and flowers!*
From *The Garden* by Andrew Marvell (1621–78)

I feel certain that anyone who has grown herbs will tell you that they soon started looking for ways to use them other than in cooking. A friend of mine has a magnificent herb garden, laid out in a traditional style, complete with lavender hedges and a centre-piece of a sun dial inscribed with Marvell's couplet (above). She grows a huge range of herbs, from everyday parsley to highly poisonous *Aconitum*, and her knowledge of herbs is extensive. Apparently her love of herbs started and was subsequently nurtured when, as a child, she visited her Grandma once a week after school for tea. Each time she visited, Grandma had prepared something containing different herbs: savoury scones with rosemary; lemon curd tarts with verbena or a piece of hand-dyed material for her to make her doll a new dress. And when she tripped and grazed her knee, Grandma had a soothing salve to make it better.

My friend became curious about how Grandma grew all these herbs and so began her 'apprenticeship', as she now calls it. She discovered which herbs were good to eat, which can be used to make a dye, which can help you relax, and which have healing properties. Under Grandma's tutelage, she also learnt how to grow herbs, starting with a few chive seeds in a pot, later taking dozens of cuttings of lavender for Grandma's new hedge, which she has now replicated in her own garden.

Not everyone has the desire, or space, to follow in my friend's size of footsteps, and many of us grow just a few herbs, such as rosemary or sage, to use in our cooking. But there are a number of common herbs that can be used in many different ways beyond the kitchen. For example, the two herbs I have just mentioned – rosemary and sage – have long been used in cosmetics and in herbal remedies. There are also many herbs that are not edible, but that can be used in the home in a variety of applications, as insect repellents or cleaners, fragrances or shampoos, or as a soothing salve or for sunburn relief.

What I would like to do in this book is to give you an insight into a number of herbs that can be used in non-culinary ways. It is by no means a comprehensive overview of all such herbs: rather it is a layperson's guide to how you can use a selection of common herbs in time-honoured but diverse ways; herbs that you may already have growing in your garden, or which are very easy to obtain.

Some of the recipes I include also call for ingredients which you are unlikely to be able to grow or produce yourself, like essential oils, for example. These are readily available from reputable suppliers, both on the high street and now also online.

What this book doesn't include is more specialised medical information – this is the domain of experts and qualified practitioners. Any suggestions for using herbs in a therapeutic, remedial or curative manner are included because, through years of empirical use, they are considered safe to use in such ways.

In Chapter One you will find some background inform-ation about how to grow your herbs, and how to harvest, preserve, and store them.

There are some herb garden designs in Chapter Two, from a basic first-aid collection to an 'anti-bug' bed.

Chapter Three looks at herbs that can be used in remedies and as first-aid applications. There are a number of easy recipes, too, so that you can make your own preparations.

Chapter Four takes us to the boudoir and bathroom, where herbs find their way into fragrant cosmetics; here you will discover how to make a natural shampoo and other treatments and treats!

Herbs for cleaning and other household uses are covered in Chapter Five: for example, there is a recipe for an all-round general cleaning fluid, and information about which herbs will keeps insects at bay, and how to keep your home smelling fragrant.

There is also a Gazetteer of selected useful herbs. This is by no means an exhaustive list but it does contain the majority of herbs that are mentioned in the text.

You will also find a Glossary which explains various terms that keep cropping up throughout this book.

# Plant Hardiness

My experience as a gardener is restricted to the British Isles; therefore all the recommendations I make and all the examples I provide in this book are based on this. The Royal Horticultural Society (RHS) introduced new hardiness classifications in 2012, which I have used in this book. I am grateful to the RHS for allowing me to reproduce the new hardiness chart, which can be found in Appendix 1.

# Latin Names

In almost all cases I have given the Latin name of the plant first with the most widely accepted common name soon after. The reason for doing this is that common names for plants can vary from region to region (a bluebell in Scotland is not the same as a bluebell in England, for example), so knowing the proper, undisputed Latin name is invaluable, especially when it comes to sourcing plants in a nursery or online. You will find a list of common names of plants and their Latin equivalents in Appendix 2.

CHAPTER I

# *Growing, Harvesting, Preserving and Storing Your Herbs*

Y ou may already grow some herbs, especially if you like to use them in cooking. But you may not know that many culinary herbs can be used in other applications. *Mentha spicata* (spearmint), for example, as well as giving your lamb an extra fillip and also aiding digestion, will repel insects; and *Rosmarinus officinalis* (rosemary), which is so often paired with chicken, has antiseptic properties and also makes a fragrant hair rinse. There are other herbs, though, that you won't have come across in your culinary endeavours, such as

1

*Saponaria officinalis* (soapwort) and *Tanacetum parthenium* (feverfew). Such herbs are well worth growing if you want to extend your knowledge and use of herbs beyond the kitchen.

Most of the herbs that are referred to in the following chapters can easily be grown in the UK. There are some, however, that will struggle in our climate – if this is the case, this will be indicated in the respective Gazetteer entry. Take note, in particular, of the hardiness rating.

Let's assume, then, that you would like to grow some herbs in your own garden. Come with me now and we'll look at the what, where and how of growing, harvesting and storing your own.

## Growing Your Herbs

### WHAT HERBS SHOULD I GROW?

Ultimately the choice is yours, but there are some herbs which are useful in all sorts of ways and perhaps these should form the basis of your collection; for example, *Chamaemelum nobile* (Roman chamomile), *Rosmarinus officinalis* (rosemary), *Thymus vulgaris* (thyme), *Calendula officinalis* (pot marigold) and *Hypericum perforatum* (St John's wort). In addition there are some herbs which are not as widely used as the ones I have already mentioned, but are, nonetheless, still worth growing: I am thinking of *Althaea officinalis* (marshmallow), *Tanacetum vulgare* (tansy) and *Plantago major* (plantain) to name but a few. In the Gazetteer you will find information about most of the herbs that are mentioned in the book.

WHERE SHOULD I GROW MY HERBS?

All herbs are best grown directly in the ground, where they can get their roots down into the soil and make strong, abundant growth. You will need to make sure that the soil conditions and the overall situation are suitable for the herbs you are growing.

Many herbs like free-draining, verging on poor, soil and a very sunny position. A number of these herbs hail from Mediterranean regions, which gives us a clue to the sort of conditions they like. Other herbs, however, like a richer soil which can retain a little more moisture, and many can cope with a little light shade. Again, you will find information about soil requirements and the optimum aspect for each of the herbs in the Gazetteer.

If your allocated space is big enough I would advise you to divide it into two main sections to accommodate the different groups and requirements.

The one thing that most herbs cannot endure is a cold wind. Try to give your herbs as much shelter from icy blasts as you can, even if it means erecting a wind break.

*Soil*

One thing that the majority of herbs have in common is that they like neutral soil. This means that the soil's pH (potential of Hydrogen) level should be in the range of 6.5 to 7. If you are not sure what pH your soil is, it is worth investing in an inexpensive testing kit that you can get from any garden centre; this will give you a reasonably accurate reading.

If your soil is slightly alkaline (this will be indicated by a slightly higher pH number), all is not lost. Most herbs will cope with these conditions. If, however, the reading is lower, it means that your soil is slightly acidic, which can be a little more problematic. If this is the case, you may need to add some lime to the soil to bring the pH level up.

If a particular herb requires soil which is not neutral, this is indicated in its entry in the Gazetteer.

### Preparing the ground

Whatever herbs you are planning to grow it is worth spending time preparing the ground before you start planting.

The most important preparation task is to make sure that the area is free of weeds. Annual weeds pose few difficulties – these can be hoed off before they have a chance to set seed, and simply left on the surface of the soil to wither or be gathered up and put on the compost heap. Do your hoeing on a dry day and when the soil surface is dry: this will prevent any sneaky weed that has somehow survived intact from taking root again.

Perennial weeds, however, may be more challenging. There are three main ways of dealing with these sorts of weeds: first, if you don't mind using chemicals, you could use a systemic herbicide. A systemic herbicide is a weed killer that you apply to the leaves of the weed. The chemicals are consequently absorbed by the plant through the leaves and taken down to the roots so that the entire plant is eventually killed off. It certainly does the job but you have to be careful not to accidentally get the weed killer on plants nearby that you don't want to get rid of.

Second, you can dig the weeds up. You have to be very watchful to get every piece of root out of the ground, though: any left in will sprout and grow.

Third, you can cover the area with something that will keep out the light – and wait. By denying the weeds one of the essential things they need to grow – in this case sunlight – they will perish naturally. Any weeds that do survive will be much weaker and easier to dig out. This method takes a little forward planning, though.

When I am preparing a new bed, I tend to combine methods two and three. I dig out as many weeds as I can but also cover the area with black plastic over the winter.

If the herbs you wish to grow are those that need a reasonably rich soil, it is as well to apply some organic matter, such as manure or compost, at the preparation stage. Spread it on the soil to a depth of about 5cm after you have cleared the weeds, but before you cover it with black plastic or some other covering. Come springtime the worms will have taken the manure or compost down into the heart of the soil and you will be left with a lovely, forkable tilth when you take off the covering.

If your herbs need really well-drained soil, make sure you incorporate some horticultural grit into the soil, and especially in the planting hole, before you plant.

To my mind the soil is of paramount importance – even more so than the position. Having said that, some herbs, such as those originating from Mediterranean climes, need a very sunny position to do well – plant them in even a part-shady position and they will languish. Most herbs, however, will just about survive, but certainly not thrive, in deep shade so try to avoid a north-facing spot.

I know of no herb that can cope with severe windy conditions, especially if they are exposed to blasts of icy wind during the dormant season. Try to choose a spot that is sheltered, or, if you have to, erect a wind break to protect your precious plants from the worst of the weather.

GROWING HERBS IN A HERB GARDEN

The *pièce de résistance* for any herb enthusiast is to have a garden solely for the purpose of growing herbs – much like my friend whom we met in the Introduction. The size of your herb garden will depend on how much space you have to spare and how many herbs you are likely to use. The expected height and, more importantly, the final spread of the herbs mentioned in this book are given in each of the Gazetteer entries, so you will be able to work out roughly how many you will be able to fit in your allocated space. There are some planting ideas in Chapter 2.

GROWING HERBS IN CONTAINERS

If you don't have space in the garden you can always grow herbs in containers. This way you can position them within easy reach and choose exactly the best spot for them in terms of aspect. You can also tailor the compost that you use to suit each herb. Generally speaking I would use soil-based compost like John Innes potting compost, rather than a peat-based one: very few herbs grow happily in peat so it doesn't make sense to fill your pots with it. A soil-based compost will also retain moisture much better, which is essential if you grow anything, not just herbs, in pots. Moisture will evaporate far more quickly from a container than from open soil, and during the growing season your pots will undoubtedly have to be watered every day – sometimes twice a day.

As a rough guide, 1cm of water will penetrate about 6–8cm of soil so you can see that, even if it rains, you will still have to top up your containers.

If the herb requires a particularly free-draining soil, add some horticultural grit or perlite to the mixture, at a rate of two or three parts compost to one part grit or perlite. (Perlite is a generic term for a naturally occurring siliceous rock which has been heat-treated to produce light, sterile granules. It has a neutral pH which means that it will not affect the acid or alkaline balance of the soil.) I tend to use perlite in containers because it is very much lighter than grit and makes the pots just that little bit easier to move around.

*What type of container shall I use?*

You can use any type of container, from a hand-crafted terracotta pot to a window box to a hanging basket to an old olive oil can. Whatever you use, make sure there are sufficient drainage holes and that the container isn't so small that the compost would dry out too quickly. Be careful, too, if you are using metal that it doesn't attract so much heat that the roots are scorched.

## HOW SHOULD I GROW MY HERBS?

Before we get to the practical nitty-gritty I would like to recommend one general method of growing herbs. I would strongly encourage you to grow your herbs organically. For the average gardener, like me, the practice of organic gardening usually means working with nature and what she provides rather than introducing man-made products such as herbicides, pesticides, artificial fertilisers, and the like. I try to dig up or hoe off weeds before they get a root-hold; I attempt to maintain a good ecological balance in my garden so that the ladybirds will eat the aphids and birds will keep the caterpillar population down to a reasonable level; and I feed the soil with a mulch of manure every year.

Although every bit of my garden is run along organic lines, it is especially important to me that whatever I use from the garden in first-aid remedies, cosmetics or in household preparations has been organically grown. I don't want any chemical residue left on the plant which may find its way into my herbal blends. Ultimately, however, it is up to you how you grow your herbs.

## BUYING POTTED HERBS

If you don't have the time, inclination or equipment to grow your own herbs, there is absolutely nothing wrong with buying herb plants from a garden centre or nursery. The best time to look for them is in late spring when new stock arrives almost weekly. (But don't be tempted to buy any of the more tender herbs – those with a hardiness rating of 3 or lower – until all risk of frost has passed.)

I would caution against buying potted herbs from supermarkets to plant in the garden. These herbs have been grown under cover, in controlled conditions, and are really only intended to be kept as 'window sill' herbs. You could try hardening them off (see page 12) before you plant them out, however, and you may be lucky.

## LABELLING

One of most important things to do when you raise your own herbs – or any other plants for that matter – is to keep tabs on exactly what it is that you are growing. There is nothing more frustrating than discovering a tray full of seedlings and having no idea what they are. When they get a little bigger you can nearly always figure out their identity, but as newly-sprungs one seedling looks very much like another. So label everything – every tray, every pot, every plant in your herb garden.

## GROWING HERBS FROM SEED

Some herbs are best grown from seed. In fact this is the only way to grow annual and biennial herbs like *Calendula officinalis* (pot marigold) and *Petroselinum crispum* (parsley) respectively.

Many other herbs can be grown from seed but sometimes germination is erratic or takes a long time – this is especially true of some of the woody herbs, such as *Lavandula angustifolia* (lavender) or *Rosmarinus officinalis* (rosemary). My general rule of thumb is that if there is a method of propagating my chosen herb other than by seed – for example, by cuttings, division, or layering – I would choose this over and above sowing seed.

Once you have succeeded in getting some plants established you can save your own seed, either to create new plants for yourself, or to give away to friends. In order to do this you have to let some of your herbs flower. As well as looking attractive, the blossoms will also benefit bees and other nectar-loving insects.

*Collecting seeds*

Collecting your own seed is very easy. The best way of deciding when seed is ripe enough to collect is to gently tap the spent flower – if the seed falls away easily then it is time.

Choose a dry, still day and equip yourself with a pair of flower snips or secateurs, and some paper bags or a tray or trays lined with newspaper. Don't use plastic as this will trap moisture and encourage decay.

Choose your seed-head and then either shake the seed into a bag or the tray, or snip off the entire head and pop it into the bag or tray to deal with later. Remember to make a note on the bag/tray of which herb seed you have collected – you are bound to forget otherwise. (I speak from experience!)

Take your collection of seed indoors and clean it by removing it from the spent flower(s) and separating it from any chaff or other bits of plant material. Then spread the seed out on a piece of kitchen paper and put it in a dry, airy room for a few days to make sure the seed is completely dry.

Pick over the seed again and remove any that are damaged. Now pop them into a dark glass jar or a stout paper envelope, label it with the name of the herb and the date on which you harvested the seed. The latter is useful to know because the older *some* seed becomes, the less likely it is to germinate.

### Sowing seeds

Seed sowing can be divided into two main methods: sowing indoors and sowing outdoors. In addition, you need to think about what time of year is best – some seeds can be sown in late summer or early autumn, when conditions for germination are still good (namely, sufficient warmth and daylight) whilst it is best to wait until spring for others. If you sow seeds late in the growing season, they will need some protection over the winter, especially if the weather is particularly cold. When you buy your herb seeds, check on the packet as to which method is best.

### Sowing seeds indoors

Indoor sowing is suitable for a whole range of herbs which can be started off and grown on inside so that they are already

11

a good size when they are planted out in the garden once the weather is warm enough.

Seeds can be sown into shallow trays and then, when they are big enough, they can be transplanted into bigger pots or they can be sown very thinly into trays with individual modules. This causes less disruption to the root system when you replant them.

Fill your container with compost and gently firm it down. It is best to water the compost at this stage: if you water after you have sown the seed, the water may wash it together, especially if the seed is very tiny. Scatter the seeds across the surface of the compost and then cover them with perlite or vermiculite, rather than compost. This will provide sufficient coverage without staying too moist. Don't forget to label the seed tray.

Now all you need to do is cover the container with clear polythene, a sheet of glass, or its own plastic cover and put it somewhere warm. Once the seeds have germinated you can remove the cover so that the seedlings have good ventilation.

When they have their first 'true' leaves you can pot the plants on into individual modules or 9-cm pots respectively, depending on whether they started off in trays or modules. As soon as they are big enough, and the risk of frost has disappeared, you can start hardening them off. This means gradually getting your babies used to the outside world. The easiest way to do this is to begin by putting them outside in a sheltered spot during the day and then bringing them back under cover at night. As the plants begin to 'toughen up' you can leave them outside all the time, but you must still give them some protection at night by covering them with some horticultural fleece. The hardening off process should take between two and three weeks, depending on the weather, by which time pesky frosts will be but a memory and the plants will be strong enough to be planted out in the garden.

*Sowing seeds outdoors*

Many seeds are best sown straight into the soil. For example, some herbs, such as *Foeniculum vulgare* (fennel), don't like their roots disturbed by transplanting, but check the instructions on your seed packet to see what is recommended. You can sow seed outdoors as long as the soil is warm and moist, and the air temperature isn't too high, which in practical terms means either in late spring or early autumn.

It's vital to have a good seedbed, free of weeds and with a fine tilth (think of the trays that you prepared for sowing indoors). With the corner of a hoe or rake make a drill, or shallow depression, in the soil, the depth of which will depend on the seed you are sowing. Generally speaking, the smaller the seed, the shallower the drill. Look at the seed packet for individual information. There you will also find out how far apart you should sow the seed and space the rows. Then water the drill. Scatter or place the seed evenly along the drill and then cover the seed with a thin layer of soil. Label the row.

You will need to check occasionally to see if the seeds need any water. If you have sown the seeds too thickly, you may need to thin them out when they are big enough. This simply means removing seedlings so that you are left with single plants, evenly spaced, with enough room between each of them so they can grow on.

## GROWING HERBS FROM CUTTINGS

There are a number of types of cuttings which can be used to increase your stock of herbs: softwood, semi-ripe, hardwood, basal, and root. Which method is best for each herb mentioned in the text is explained in the individual entry in the Gazetteer.

Take heed if you take cuttings, though. Don't expect all your cuttings to 'take', namely to produce new roots and shoots. Some will inevitably die before they have a chance to live, as it were, so don't be disappointed if you lose a good number. I nearly always prepare twice as many cuttings as the number of plants I want to end up with – my success rate is generally better than 50 per cent but it's best to be on the safe side. I give away any spare plants and make lots of new friends as a result!

### Softwood cuttings

You can take softwood cuttings in late spring and early summer. Material is taken from the soft and flexible young shoot tips, which root readily at this time of year. The best time of day to do this is in the morning when the plant is turgid, or full of water.

Before you start taking cuttings, make sure you have a clean, sharp knife and have ready some clean, 9-cm pots filled with compost. The number of pots depends on how many cuttings you wish to take: you can fit four or five in a pot. Select a non-flowering shoot and cut it just above where the leaves join the stem – the node. You need a shoot about 10cm long. Pop the shoots into a plastic bag until you are ready to prepare them for planting: this will prevent them from wilting.

When you are ready to plant them, take the cuttings out of the plastic bag and, with a sharp knife, cut the bottom of the shoot off to just below a node. Carefully remove the lower leaves and pinch out the top of the shoot. Then make a hole in the pot of compost near to the edge – you can use a dibber, but I use a pencil, which seems to do just as good a job – pop the cutting in so that the first set of leaves is above the surface of the compost and push the compost back around the cutting. Water the pot from above so that the compost settles around the cutting. Label the pot.

If you have a heated propagator this is ideal for your cuttings, but I pop each pot into a large plastic freezer bag and use the thin paper-coated wire tie to loosely pull the opening together at the top. I don't tie it tightly, but leave a small gap so that a certain amount of air can still circulate. The whole thing then goes on the window sill, and because the pot is inside the bag, you don't need to worry about standing the pot on a saucer. Don't put the pot in direct sunlight, though, as this will scorch the leaves. Open up the bag periodically to aid ventilation and remove any dead or decaying material as you see it. Keep the compost moist.

Once the cuttings are well rooted you can pot them on into their own individual containers. As long as you can do this by mid-summer they will develop enough roots to carry them through the dormant season; otherwise leave them and pot them on early in the next growing season.

### Semi-ripe cuttings

Late summer or early autumn is the time to take semi-ripe cuttings. These are cuttings from the current season's growth where the base of the cutting is hard while the tip is still soft. The method for taking semi-ripe cuttings is just the same as for softwood cuttings, above.

### Hardwood cuttings

It is important to remember to take hardwood cuttings during the dormant season, when the plant is not growing. The ideal time is just after the leaves have fallen in the autumn or during late winter to early spring just before the new buds start to burst. To take hardwood cuttings you should choose a shoot that has grown in the current year. Remove any soft growth at the tip. You should make a sloping cut just above a bud at the top, and a straight cut just below a bud at the base – this way you know which way up you should plant the cutting. Both roots and shoots will break from the dormant buds so the more buds there are, the shorter the cutting can be.

You can plant hardwood cuttings into a trench outdoors but I always put mine into pots filled with a mixture of 50 per cent horticultural grit and 50 per cent multi-purpose compost. Water them in and leave them in a sheltered position in the garden (a cold frame is ideal but not a necessity). Don't worry if nothing appears to be happening for some time after you have planted your cuttings; it usually takes a while for them to develop roots and shoots and it may be well into the new growing season before anything starts to occur.

*Basal cuttings*

Sometimes you will see new shoots growing from the crown, or base, of the herb. These will make excellent cuttings. Cut a shoot about 7.5–10cm long from the parent herb and then treat it as a softwood cutting (see above).

*Root cuttings*

You can take root cuttings during the dormant season. First, fill a seed tray with gritty compost, press it down slightly and water it. Then carefully dig up the parent plant, keeping intact as much root as possible. With a sharp knife cut off vigorous roots as close to the crown as you can, but do not remove more than a third of the root system from the parent plant otherwise it will struggle when you replant it. Cut each root into 3–10cm lengths (the thinner the root, the longer the cuttings should be), place the lengths on the surface of the prepared tray about 4cm apart, and cover them with a thin layer of compost. Label the tray.

Place your root cuttings in a sheltered position – again a

cold frame is ideal – and in the following early growing season, when there are signs of growth, and when the cuttings are well rooted, pot them up individually to grow on.

*Cuttings in water*

One of the easiest methods of making new plants is by stripping off the bottom leaves of a stem – as you would when taking a cutting – and immersing the stripped part in water rather than compost. Roots will soon start to appear at the nodes (the leaf joints). You should change the water every day to prevent the growth of damaging bacteria. As soon as the roots are about 1cm long you should pot up the new plant.

This method doesn't work with all herbs, but it is certainly a fail-safe way of propagating any *Mentha* species (mints) as well as *Ocimum* species (basil) and *Melissa officinalis* (lemon balm).

### LAYERING

Another method of propagation which works for some herbs is layering. You need a good, strong, established plant for this, and one which has a tendency to allow some of its stems to droop to the ground, such as *Thymus* species (thyme).

The best time to layer a herb is in late spring or early summer when the soil is warm. Remove all weeds from where you want your new 'plant' to grow and dig over the soil so you have a good tilth. Now take a long stem from the parent plant, and remove any leaves and side shoots, taking care not to damage the growing tip. On one side of the stem, scrape a little of the outer layer away and ease the stem, exposed side down, to the ground. Now pin the stem in place with a piece of wire (I use a piece of cut-up wire coat hanger about 15cm long which I have bent double into a u-shape) so that the stem is in contact with the soil. Cover the stem with soil, making sure that the growing tip remains above ground. Water in well and let nature take its course.

Some layered herbs will root by late autumn, in which case you should sever the new plant from its parent and pot it up to spend the dormant season in a cold frame or similar environment. If the stem has not produced roots by late autumn, leave it until the following year.

DIVISION

A further technique of increasing your plant numbers is by division. This simply means taking an existing plant and splitting it into pieces.

The process of division is very straightforward: carefully dig up the plant, trying not to damage too many roots, and shake off as much soil as possible. Then all you have to do is to divide the plant into sections, making sure that each section has three to five healthy shoots. Sometimes you can tease the clumps apart with your hands. Some plants, however, require something a little more vigorous and you may need to use a sharp knife to slice the plant into sections. It will become clear as you do it which technique you will need to use.

Once you have your new clumps you can plant them straight away, making sure you water them in well. If you don't want to plant them in the ground immediately, you can pot them up individually and keep them until required – again make sure they are well-watered.

STOLONS OR SUCKERS

A stolon is a stem from the mother plant that grows at, or just below, the soil surface, and forms roots of its own. A new plant, known as a sucker, will then develop. The most obvious example of this form of growth is found in *Fragaria* species (strawberry).

To take advantage of the availability of these 'plants for free', cut the stolon, then carefully loosen the soil around the sucker with a fork and lift the whole thing, roots and all, being careful not to damage the mother plant. Trim both the sucker portion and the mother plant portion back to the fibrous roots of each.

Reduce any leafy shoots of the sucker by about half and then plant it out in the garden or pot it up to grow on. Make sure you water it regularly during its first season of 'going it alone'.

This type of propagation is best done in spring.

PLANTING OUT

When the time comes to plant out your herbs – which in practical terms means after the frosts have gone in late spring, and before they come again in the autumn – there is a little bit of preparation to do first.

Firstly, if your plants have been given protection they need to be hardened off. (See page 120)

Assuming that the area is weed-free, all you need to do is lightly fork over the soil and dig a hole slightly larger than the size of the pot. If the herb you are planting needs good drainage, you can put a good layer of horticultural grit in the bottom of the hole and mix some in with the rest of the dug-out soil before you backfill. Firm the plant in and, even if the soil is moist, give it a good watering.

How far apart you plant your herbs depends on their eventual spread, so check this first in the Gazetteer – too far apart and they look abandoned; too close together and they will become overcrowded.

## HOW CAN I KEEP MY HERBS GROWING WELL AND LOOKING GOOD?

### Weeds

Try to keep on top of the weeding so that your precious herbs have as little competition as possible. Little and often is the best way, I have found. In fact, I think there is something almost therapeutic about allocating a certain amount of time on a regular basis for the weeding: it takes little concentration and you can let your mind wander in a way that few other tasks allow.

*Water*

I only water my herbs in the garden when I have just planted them and then during the first growing season if they are showing signs of stress. Otherwise they have to fend for themselves.

Herbs in containers are a different matter – they require watering at least once a day during the growing season, less often during the dormant season.

Many people maintain that you should only water in the early morning or evening. These are certainly the optimum times, but if you see your plants flagging during the middle of the day, water them – by evening it may be too late! If it is a particularly sunny day avoid splashing water onto the leaves however; water droplets act like little magnifying glasses and the leaves may be scorched, so water the soil, not the plant.

*Mulch/feed*

In order to retain moisture, keep weeds down and feed the soil, I have developed the practice of applying mulch at least once a year. Mulching simply means spreading a layer of organic matter, such as compost, on the surface of the soil, taking care not to cover any crowns or soft areas of growth. If the herbs are greedy feeders I give them a generous portion, sometimes second helpings: if on the other hand they prefer nutrient-poor soil, I keep mulching to a minimum, offering them just a very meagre, Oliver Twist-size helping.

If you are growing herbs in containers, you will have to feed them during the main growing season to keep them healthy. A liquid seaweed fertiliser, applied according to the instructions on the bottle, is ideal for this. You could also use a slow-release fertiliser – you can buy this as small, round granules (which look a bit like slug eggs when they are incorporated into the mixture!) or as compacted 'plugs'. This type of food will last for several months so the best time to add it to the soil is in late spring, especially if you are potting up new plants or re-potting established ones.

*Prune/cut back*
This should be unnecessary if you harvest your herbs regularly. If, however, you see any dead or dying growth, remove it immediately to prevent disease and to encourage new growth.

*Support*
A few tall-growing or sprawling herbs may require some support. A stake, such as a stout bamboo cane, may be all that is needed for the tall-growing ones, such as *Verbascum thrapsus* (mullein) which has flowers carried on a rocketing central stem. Others, such as *Borago officinalis* (borage), can slump a little if they get too 'leggy': these can easily be contained by means of four or five short bamboo canes spaced around the plant with garden twine laced between to form a corral – this will keep them upright and confined.

*Pinch out flowers/dead head*

Unless you want a herb to flower in order to use the flowers themselves, to feed beneficial insects, or to set seed, it is a good idea to pinch out the flowering tips at regular intervals. This means that any energy that would have been directed into producing flowers is now diverted by the plant into building up an abundance of leaves.

Similarly, if you have allowed your herbs to flower but do not wish to collect seed, snip off the dead blooms to encourage further growth.

# Harvesting Your Herbs

What you harvest from a herb plant depends on what herb it is. For example, in some cases you use only the leaves; from other herbs you will need the flowers or roots. So let's look now at when and how you should gather each part of the plant.

WHEN SHOULD I HARVEST MY HERBS?

*Leaves*

If you want to use the leaves immediately, harvest them as and when you need them, but preferably before the plant has flowered – this is when the flavour in the leaves is most intense. This is certainly the case during the summer months when all herbs are in full leaf. Many herbs like *Rosmarinus officinalis* (rosemary), *Hyssopus officinalis* (hyssop), and *Thymus vulgaris* (thyme) are evergreen and can be harvested all year round if you want to use them fresh.

For soft-stemmed herbs you can use a pair of kitchen scissors but you may find secateurs are needed for some of the woody ones. I use a pair of flower snips which are half-way between the two: they can cope with all but the thickest of sprigs. Never cut more than a third of the growing stems at any one time: although annual herbs will grow back fairly quickly, perennial ones take longer to recover.

If you cut a few hours or even a couple of days in advance, treat them as you would cut flowers: recut the stems and strip off the lower leaves just before plunging them into a jar or vase of fresh water and replace the water each day.

If you are harvesting leaves in order to dry or preserve them in some other way, pick them in dry weather after any dew has evaporated but before the heat of the midday sun. Very few of the essential oils in the leaves will have evaporated and the drying or preserving process will proceed better if there is no moisture on the leaves.

*Flowers and petals*
Like the leaves, you should pick flowers when the dew has evaporated and before the heat of the sun. Most flowers are at their best when they have just opened. Pick individual flowers, such as *Rosa* species (rose), or inflorescences, like *Sambucus nigra* (elder), with their stalks: the stalks can be removed after picking. In some cases, like *Calendula officinalis* (pot marigold), you only use the petals – again pick the whole flower and separate the petals later.

*Seeds*

If you want to harvest seeds to use in your preparations you should gather them in just the same way as you would if you were collecting them to grow into plants (see page 10). You will have to be more careful at the cleaning stage, however, because you only want to keep the seeds. It is painstaking but necessary work.

*Roots, rhizomes and tubers*

These are harvested during the autumn, usually after any above-ground parts have died down. If you only want to use a portion of the underground part, you can carefully dig up the entire root, rhizome or tuber, remove as much as you need, and then replant the remainder.

Wash off any soil and the root is ready to use or preserve.

*Bulbs*

Very few bulbs are used in the herbal preparations in this book. In fact the only bulb in my collection of herbs is *Allium sativum* (garlic). It is said that you should plant your cloves of garlic on the shortest day, and harvest them on the longest day of the year. In practice this doesn't always work out. I wait until the foliage starts to turn yellow, then I dig up the bulbs, being careful not to bruise them.

Because I can never be certain of having a long spell of dry weather after I have dug my garlic bulbs, I take them indoors and lay them on a wire mesh frame that I made for

26

the purpose. (It's simply a square of timber with chicken wire stretched over it and tacked to the frame.) I leave the garlic for about 3 or 4 weeks and then cut off the dried roots and, if the dried foliage and stems are long enough, I plait them together to form a 'rope' of garlic bulbs, or, if the stems are too short, I pop individual bulbs in a netting bag.

Store the bulbs in a dry, frost-free place. The temperature must not be allowed to rise above 4°C otherwise the bulbs will start to shoot. Check them periodically to make sure they haven't turned mouldy or started to rot.

FORAGING FROM THE WILD

Some herbs can be harvested from the wild; however, there are a few points that you need to bear in mind before you go out armed with scissors and secateurs.

First, you have to be absolutely sure what it is that you are harvesting. This may be an obvious thing to say but some plants look very similar – in particular, I am thinking of the Apiaceae family whose members include the benign *Daucus carota* (carrot) but also the deadly *Conium maculatum* (hemlock). If you are in any doubt at all, leave the plant alone.

Second, make sure that what you intend to gather is not a protected species. You can find the relevant information at www.jncc.defra.gov.uk.

Third, make sure that it is legal to gather from your harvesting location. Usually, gathering foliage, fruit and flowers from road verges and hedgerows accessible from the road is permissible. However, you are not allowed to uproot any plant without the landowner's permission, even if it is growing on 'public' land. If you want to harvest something from any other 'private' site, a farmer's field for example, or an area adjacent to a public footpath, you must get the landowner's permission first.

I remember an occasion when I was up on the fells with my beekeeping friend and the owner of the land. My friend was looking for somewhere to put his hives so the bees could forage on the local heather, and the landowner was pointing out various places that might be suitable. While this was going on, a couple of ladies were happily, and busily, gathering bilberries that were growing some way from the public footpath which dissects the land.

After our beekeeping discussion had ended the landowner took a bag out of her pocket, went up to the ladies, politely thanked them for gathering the berries on her behalf, relieved them of their harvest, and suggested that next time they should ask her permission before they strayed onto her land! The two ladies were totally dumbfounded and stood, open-mouthed. The landowner was well within her rights, of course, and the two ladies were well off their right of way.

There are some areas that you are not allowed to gather from at all; for example, some spaces have been earmarked as Sites of Special Scientific Interest (SSSI) or have a similar designation and on no account should you gather anything from them. If you are in any doubt, check with your local authority.

Fourth, be wary of where you are gathering from. I have

mentioned road verges, but these are probably some of the worst places because of the potential contamination from vehicle exhausts and so on. Also be aware of any areas that look as if they have been chemically treated in some way, for example, with weed killer.

Fifth, only harvest what you need and never strip one plant entirely. Always leave some foliage and flowers so that the plant can regenerate, and never take all the fruit: other species rely on the harvest as their sole source of food at that time of year.

Sixth, respect the environment that you are harvesting from and never disturb nesting birds.

Seventh, always wash your bounty (no, not the coconut and chocolate bar!) before you use it. You never know how many incontinent creatures have been scuttling through it!

With all that in mind – happy foraging!

## Preserving Your Herbs

FREEZING

One way of preserving your herbs is by freezing them. This method works with a variety of leaves, flowers and roots, although some leaves and fleshy roots tend to soften to a mush when they thaw; trial and error is the order of the day with these. Harvest the parts you want to freeze, and, as soon as possible after harvesting, chop them and pack them into ice cube trays: this is an ideal 'portion' which can be used when you have no fresh herbs available. Fast freeze them immediately.

DRYING

A number of herbs are suitable for drying. Indeed, many recipes for the kind of preparations we are making in this book call for dried herbs. The idea here is to eliminate all the water content from the leaves, flowers, petals, stems or roots.

*Drying aerial parts*

In order to dry leaves, flowers, and other bits that grow above ground level, I have a rack which is simply a piece of muslin stretched over a wooden frame – this allows for good circulation of air. Space the leaves, flowers, petals or stalks on the muslin and put the rack in a dark, warm, dry place until the plant parts are completely desiccated – this can take up to three days.

You can also hang bunches of herbs upside down to dry. Again, good air circulation is vital. The ideal temperature for both methods is 20–32°C. If any herbs develop mould or turn black, discard them because they will not keep.

*Drying underground parts*

Because roots and the like are much tougher than aerial parts, you can dry them in an oven. Make sure the roots are completely clean and dry, cut them into small pieces and lay them on a baking tray. Pop them in the oven on a very low heat (50–60°C – reduce the temperature by 10°C if you have a fan oven) until they are completely dried out. This will take between two and three hours, depending on the herb and the sizes of the individual plant parts.

## Storing Your Herbs

Once you have dried your herbs, the last thing you want is for them to reabsorb any moisture so you need to find containers which will exclude as much air as possible without encouraging any humidity.

By far the best type of container is a dark glass jar with a tight-fitting lid. Dark glass reduces the amount of light reaching the herbs and therefore helps to prevent bleaching and oxidation. This way your herbs will keep longer. If you can't get hold of jars with dark glass, use clear ones, but be sure to keep them in a dark cupboard away from sunlight. Use jars that are just big enough for the volume of herbs you are storing – too much 'air space' will encourage deterioration.

Once you have put your herbs into the jars, be sure to add a label showing exactly what the herb is and the date you picked it.

Your dried herbs should last up to a year, but if mould forms or if they show any other signs of spoiling you should discard them immediately.

CHAPTER 2

## *Planting Plans*

I n this chapter you will find 6 planting plans covering some the various uses of herbs that I am looking at in this book:

- Maureen's 'Desert Island' bed
- A 'basic' first-aid bed
- Some more first-aid herbs
- A cosmetic herb bed
- A fragrant herb bed
- An 'anti-bug' bed
- A dye bed

Each plan is a 'module' measuring 2 metres by 1 metre and is designed so that you can create a series of beds, depending on what your herbal interest is, and how much space you have available in your garden. So, for example, if you have an area measuring 2 metres by 2 metres, you could have an area for first-aid herbs alongside one for fragrant herbs.

If you do link beds together, it is a good idea to allow space for a path between the beds for easy access. A series of stepping-stone paving slabs is ideal: this would give you the opportunity you to plant some additional low-growing herbs, such as *Thymus* species (thyme) between the slabs.

OMISSIONS

You will notice that some very useful herbs have not been included in any of the plans. This is deliberate. Some herbs, such as *Mentha* species (mint) and *Symphytum officinale* (comfrey), tend to be invasive if left to their own devices in the garden, so I grow them in pots in order to keep their wayward behaviour in check! Others, such as *Hamamelis virginiana* (witch-hazel) and *Sambucus nigra* (elder), are too large to include in such a modest space – these are best grown as part of a larger garden scheme. And there are those plants which are so common in the wild, or inveigle themselves, unbidden, into the garden, that it would be false economy to include them in a garden location – these include herbs such as *Equisetum arvense* (horsetail) and *Urtica dioica* (nettle).

# Maureen's 'Desert Island' Bed

No, I don't mean these herbs need a desert island to grown on! These are the ones that I couldn't do without. I thought long and hard about which herbs I would include in a 'must-have' bed measuring only 2 metres by 1 metre: it was a hard decision, but the ones I have chosen crop up time and again in the preparations I use. You will no doubt have your own favourites, but I think this choice is a good starting point.

NO. OF PLANTS REQUIRED

| | |
|---|---|
| *Calendula officinalis* (pot marigold) | 5 |
| *Chamaemelum nobile* (Roman chamomile) | 3 |
| or *Matricaria recutita* (German chamomile) | |
| *Lavandula angustifolia* (lavender) | 1 |
| *Rosa gallica* var. *officinalis* (Apothecary's rose) | 1 |
| *Rosmarinus officinalis* (rosemary) | 1 |
| *Salvia officinalis* (sage) | 2 |
| *Thymus vulgaris* (thyme) | 2 |

All these herbs are perennial apart from *Calendula officinalis* (pot marigold), which is an annual and will have to be replaced each year. The easiest way for you to ensure you have plants year on year is to collect some seed from your plants in the autumn and either sow it immediately, or save it until spring.

*Chamaemelum nobile* (Roman chamomile) (or *Matricaria recutita* (German chamomile) if you prefer), *Lavandula angustifolia* (lavender), *Rosmarinus officinalis* (rosemary),

*Calendula officinalis*
(pot marigold)

*Rosmarinus officinalis*
(rosemary)

*Rosa gallica*
var. *officinalis* (rose)

*Thymus vulgaris*
(thyme)

*Salvia officinalis*
(sage)

*Lavandula angustifolia* (lavender)

*Chamaemelum nobile* (Roman chamomile)
or *Matricaria recutita*
(German chamomile)

*Salvia officinalis* (sage) and *Thymus vulgaris* (thyme) all require quite free-draining soil, so when you plant these herbs, incorporate a generous amount of horticultural grit into the planting hole and back fill.

*Rosa gallica* var. *officinalis* (Apothecary's rose) will benefit from a good amount of well-rotted manure added to the planting hole, as well as a mulch of the same each year.

# Basic First-aid Bed

This module includes some of the most commonly used herbs for first-aid.

NO. OF PLANTS REQUIRED

| | |
|---|---|
| *Calendula officinalis* (pot marigold) | 8 |
| *Chamaemelum nobile* (Roman chamomile) | 4 |
| or *Matricaria recutita* (German chamomile) | |
| *Hypericum perforatum* (St John's wort) | 1 |
| *Lavandula angustifolia* (lavender) | 1 |
| *Rosmarinus officinalis* (rosemary) | 1 |
| *Salvia officinalis* (sage) | 4 |
| *Thymus vulgaris* (thyme) | 2 |

The only annual plant amongst the perennials is *Calendula officinalis* (pot marigold) which will have to be replaced each year. *Chamaemelum nobilis* (Roman chamomile) (or *Matricaria recutita* (German chamomile) if you prefer), *Lavandula angustifolia* (lavender), *Rosmarinus officinalis*

Planting Plans

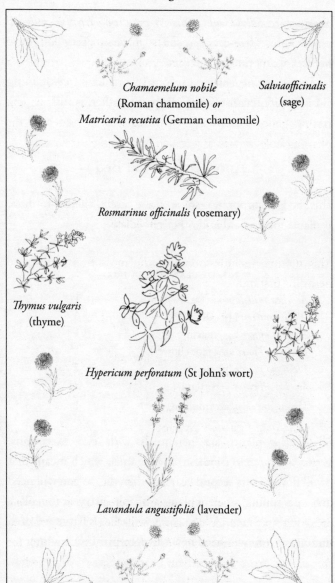

*Chamaemelum nobile*
(Roman chamomile) *or*
*Matricaria recutita* (German chamomile)

*Salviaofficinalis*
(sage)

*Rosmarinus officinalis* (rosemary)

*Thymus vulgaris*
(thyme)

*Hypericum perforatum* (St John's wort)

*Lavandula angustifolia* (lavender)

37

(rosemary), *Salvia officinalis* (sage) and *Thymus vulgaris* (thyme) prefer free-draining soil, so make sure they don't have wet feet at any time of the year.

*Hypericum perforatum* (St John's wort) likes free-draining but moisture retentive soil – average in other words!

## Another First-aid Bed

This bed incorporates some more useful herbs to have available for first-aid and other remedies.

NO. OF PLANTS REQUIRED

| | |
|---|---|
| *Achillea millefolium* (yarrow) | 1 |
| *Allium sativum* (garlic) | 6 |
| *Althaea officinalis* (marshmallow) | 1 |
| *Echinacea purpurea* (coneflower) | 1 |
| *Plantago major* (plantain) | 2 |
| *Stachys officinalis* (betony) | 2 |
| *Verbascum thrapsus* (mullein) | 1 |

All of the plants are perennials with two exceptions. *Verbascum thrapsus* (mullein) is a biennial, which means that it will flower in its second year and then die, so you will need to have a 'rolling' stock of plants available each year to replace the dying specimen. *Allium sativum* (garlic) is harvested each summer so you will need new cloves to plant each winter.

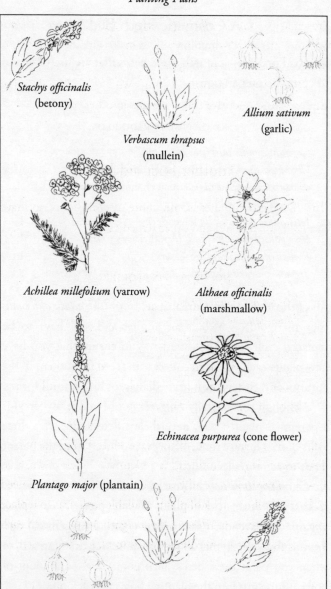

*Stachys officinalis* (betony)

*Verbascum thrapsus* (mullein)

*Allium sativum* (garlic)

*Achillea millefolium* (yarrow)

*Althaea officinalis* (marshmallow)

*Echinacea purpurea* (cone flower)

*Plantago major* (plantain)

# A Cosmetic Herb Bed

This bed provides you with some herbs that are useful to add to cosmetic preparations.

NO. OF PLANTS REQUIRED

| | |
|---|---|
| *Calendula officinalis* (pot marigold) | 4 |
| *Chamaemelum nobile* (Roman chamomile) | 4 |
| or *Matricaria recutita* (German chamomile) | |
| *Fragaria vesca* (wild strawberry) | 4 |
| *Lavandula angustifolia* (lavender) | 1 |
| *Rosa gallica* var. *officinalis* (Apothecary's rose) | 1 |
| *Rosmarinus officinalis* (rosemary) | 1 |
| *Thymus vulgaris* (thyme) | 2 |

All of the herbs are perennial apart from *Calendula officinalis* (pot marigold), which is an annual and will have to be replaced each year. The easiest way to ensure that you have new plants each year is to collect some seed from them in the autumn and either sow it immediately, or save it until spring.

Although theoretically *Fragaria vesca* (wild strawberry) is a perennial plant it will, nevertheless deteriorate after three years or so. Nurture some offspring produced from the parent plant to act as replacements.

*Chamaemelum nobile* (Roman chamomile) (or *Matricaria recutita* (German chamomile) if you prefer), *Lavandula angustifolia* (lavender), *Rosmarinus officinalis* (rosemary) and *Thymus vulgaris* (thyme) all require quite free-draining soil, so when you plant these herbs, incorporate a good amount of horticultural grit into the planting hole and back fill.

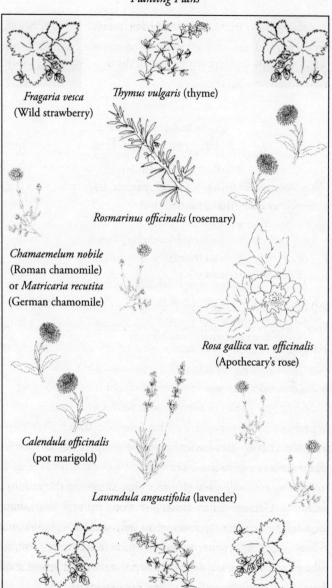

*Fragaria vesca*
(Wild strawberry)

*Thymus vulgaris* (thyme)

*Rosmarinus officinalis* (rosemary)

*Chamaemelum nobile*
(Roman chamomile)
or *Matricaria recutita*
(German chamomile)

*Rosa gallica* var. *officinalis*
(Apothecary's rose)

*Calendula officinalis*
(pot marigold)

*Lavandula angustifolia* (lavender)

*Rosa gallica* var. *officinalis* (Apothecary's rose) will benefit from a good amount of well-rotted manure added to the planting hole, as well as a mulch of the same each year.

# A Fragrant Herb Bed

These herbs will bring beautiful, natural fragrances into your home – so ditch the aerosol!

### NO. OF PLANTS REQUIRED

| | |
|---|---|
| *Galium odoratum* (sweet woodruff) | 2 |
| *Iris germanica* var. *florentina* (iris) | 2 |
| *Lavandula angustifolia* (lavender) | 2 |
| *Pelargonium capitatum* (rose-scented pelargonium) | 4 |
| *Rosa gallica* var. *officinalis* (Apothecary's rose) | 1 |
| *Salvia officinalis* (sage) | 2 |

All the herbs are hardy perennials apart from one – *Pelargonium capitatum* (rose-scented pelargonium). This is tender so you will have to dig up the plants in the autumn before the onset of any frost, pot them up and keep them in a frost-free place over winter so they can be replanted the following year. It is also a good idea to take softwood cuttings (see page 14) periodically to replace the parent plants if they become too woody and lose their floriferousness.

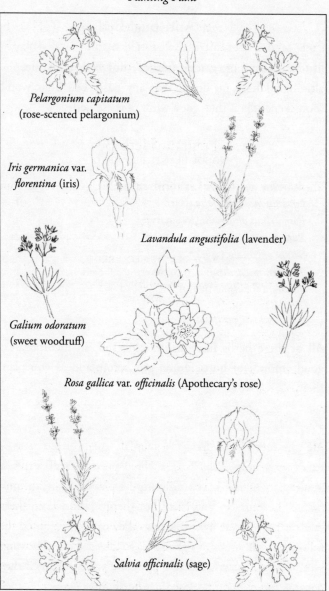

*Pelargonium capitatum*
(rose-scented pelargonium)

*Iris germanica* var.
*florentina* (iris)

*Lavandula angustifolia* (lavender)

*Galium odoratum*
(sweet woodruff)

*Rosa gallica* var. *officinalis* (Apothecary's rose)

*Salvia officinalis* (sage)

# An 'Anti-bug' Bed

This is bed as in 'garden border', not bed as in 'sleep' –
although I have no doubt that any nasty bed bugs would
soon skedaddle if they got a whiff of these herbs!

NO. OF PLANTS REQUIRED

| | |
|---|---|
| *Artemisia abrotanum* (southernwood) | 2 |
| *Lavandula angustifolia* (lavender) | 1 |
| *Rosmarinus officinalis* (rosemary) | 1 |
| *Ruta graveoloens* (rue) | 2 |
| *Salvia officinalis* (sage) | 2 |
| *Tanacetum parthenium* (feverfew) | 1 |
| *Tanacetum vulgare* (tansy) | 1 |

All of these herbs like free-draining soil, so incorporate a
good amount of horticultural grit before and as you plant
them.

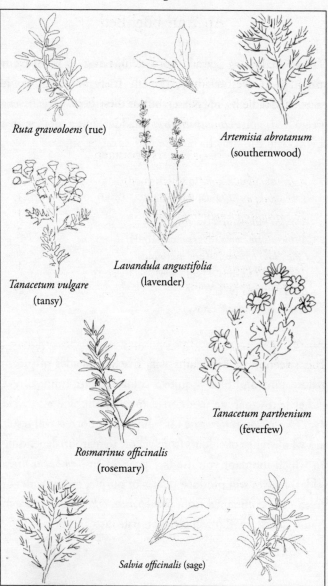

*Ruta graveoloens* (rue)

*Artemisia abrotanum*
(southernwood)

*Tanacetum vulgare*
(tansy)

*Lavandula angustifolia*
(lavender)

*Tanacetum parthenium*
(feverfew)

*Rosmarinus officinalis*
(rosemary)

*Salvia officinalis* (sage)

# A Dye Bed

This bed contains a small, but useful, range of herbs from which good dyes can be obtained. There are many more excellent dye herbs, of course, such as *Genista tinctoria* (dyer's greenweed) and *Rubia tinctorum* (madder) but a modest area such as this can only be home to a few select ones.

#### NO. OF PLANTS REQUIRED

| | |
|---|---|
| *Achillea millefolium* (yarrow) | 1 |
| *Anthemis tinctoria* (dyer's chamomile) | 1 |
| *Calendula officinalis* (pot marigold) | 5 |
| *Carthamus tinctorius* (safflower) | 1 |
| *Isatis tinctoria* (woad) | 2 |
| *Tanacetum vulgare* (tansy) | 1 |

This selection of dye plants will give you shades of green, yellow, pink and blue – quite a colour palette from so few. Other herbs that are mentioned in the book will also yield dye: *Hypericum perforatum* (St John's wort) flowers will result in a whole range of colours from yellow to maroon depending on which mordant you use (see page 112); *Sambucus nigra* (elder) berries will produce shades of purple; more shades of green can be obtained from *Symphytum officinale* (comfrey); *Urtica dioica* (nettle) will give you pale tans and beige.

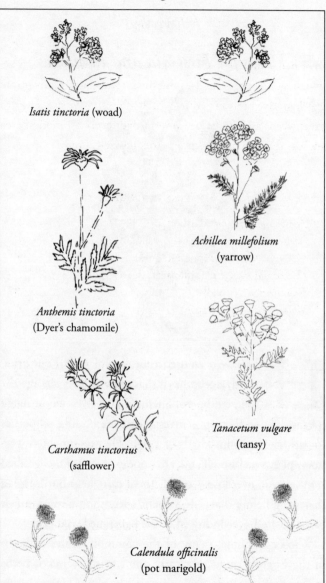

*Isatis tinctoria* (woad)

*Achillea millefolium*
(yarrow)

*Anthemis tinctoria*
(Dyer's chamomile)

*Tanacetum vulgare*
(tansy)

*Carthamus tinctorius*
(safflower)

*Calendula officinalis*
(pot marigold)

## CHAPTER 3

# *Herbs for First-aid and Remedies*

Herbs have been used as healing plants for centuries. Indeed, legend has it that some 5,000 years ago the Chinese Emperor Shennong (神农) – whose name means 'Divine Farmer' – investigated the healing properties (or otherwise) of hundreds of herbs. He experimented with many plants on himself and, after one experiment too far, died from a toxic overdose – oops! And I can't help but imagine that, long before that, Mr Sapiens chewed on a mint leaf or two after he'd over-indulged in the barbecued wild boar.

Closer to home, many of the common names of herbs in the English language clearly point to the value of herbs to support healing: for example, knitbone (*Symphytum officinale*) and self-heal (*Prunella vulgaris*). Until relatively recently, in every village, if not in every family, there would be someone – usually a 'wise' woman, or for those who were a little more superstitious and ungenerous, the local 'witch' – who would have a comprehensive knowledge of the herbs required to ease ailments and aid healing.

Although much of the understanding about herbs, and the many related skills, is no longer common knowledge, there is still a vestige of awareness of the potential of herbs. For example, many of us know that the juice of the *Aloe vera* plant will ease sunburn, and that a cup of *Chamaemelum nobile* (Roman chamomile) tea will aid sleep. Applications such as these, like the ones I offer in this book, are safe for the layperson to use because they have been tried and tested over generations. It almost goes without saying, however – but I shall reiterate it anyway – that *some herbs can be unsafe, even dangerous, if the person using them does not have specialist knowledge. If you have any doubts at all, you must seek professional guidance.*

Pregnant or lactating women should also seek professional advice before taking or using *any* of the remedies.


COMMON AILMENTS

I have listed, in alphabetical order, some common ailments which may benefit from a herbal ministration. As well as topical treatments, I have, where appropriate, included a recipe which will not only help ease the symptoms but will taste good too!

I have not included disorders such as depression, stress or

high blood pressure – these need professional diagnosis and should not be treated by a layperson.

ACHING MUSCLES

There is no doubt that a massage can help relieve aching muscles, and if the oil that you use has been infused (see page 190) with some appropriate herbs it can be even more efficacious. Almond oil makes a good base but any vegetable oil is acceptable. Use *Rosmarinus officinalis* (rosemary), which will stimulate blood flow, *Hypericum perforatum* (St John's wort) to ease muscle tension, and *Chamaemelum nobile* (Roman chamomile), which will act as an anti-inflammatory.

We all know how much a soak in a warm bath can help ease aching muscles. Add some herbs and essential oils and it is even more worthwhile. Here are two suggestions – the first is ideal for someone who doesn't particularly want to come up smelling of roses!

*Rosemary and Lemon Balm Bath Infusion*

You will need:

4 teaspoons fresh *Melissa officinalis* (lemon balm)

2 teaspoons fresh *Rosmarinus officinalis* (rosemary) leaves

3 drops of lemon balm essential oil

Make an infusion (see page 190) using the fresh lemon balm and rosemary leaves and 500ml water. When the infusion is cold, add the essential oil and use it immediately in your warm bath.

*Rose and Chamomile Bath Infusion*

You will need:

2 teaspoons dried *Rosa gallica* var. *officinalis* (Apothecary's rose) petals

2 teaspoons of dried *Chamaemelum nobile* (Roman chamomile) or *Matricaria recutita* (German chamomile) flowers

3 drops of rose essential oil

Make an infusion (see page 190) using the rose petals and chamomile flowers and 500ml water. When the infusion is cold, add the essential oil and pour it into your freshly run bath.

ACNE

Acne, the bane of many a hormonal teenager's life, is caused when the skin's sebaceous glands become blocked. One way of alleviating the symptoms is to use a herb-rich facial wash morning and evening. Make an infusion (see page 190) using *Tropaeolum majus* (nasturtium) and *Borago officinalis* (borage) leaves and flowers, *Fragaria vesca* (strawberry) leaves, *Lavandula angustifolia* (lavender) flowers and *Sambucus nigra* (elder) flowers, and use as a face wash or on cotton wool as a cleanser.

You can also enjoy this warming soup, packed with vegetables and herbs that contain nutrients, such as Vitamin A and anti-inflammatories, which promote healthy skin.

*Carrot, Ginger and Fennel Soup*

You will need:

1 tablespoon olive oil

450g carrots, cleaned and cut into chunks

1 large onion, peeled and chopped

2 small potatoes, peeled and cut into chunks

5 cloves garlic, peeled and finely chopped

5cm piece of root ginger, peeled and finely chopped

1.5 ltrs vegetable stock

Leaves of about 10 sprigs of fennel

Salt and pepper to taste

Heat the oil in a saucepan and add the onion, garlic and ginger. Sauté them until the onion starts to soften. Add the other vegetables along with the stock and bring to the boil. Cover and simmer for about 20 minutes until the carrots are very soft.

Take off the heat, add the fennel leaves and blend until smooth.

APATHY

Every now and again we all feel a bit apathetic. This is when it feels as if all your 'get up and go' has already got up and gone – or as a friend of mine says: 'the bounce has gone from my bungee'. This type of 'feeling down' should not be confused with depression, which often has deep-rooted causes requiring professional skill and time to identify. Indeed, it often takes the sufferer some time to realise and acknowledge that what they are feeling is unusual for them. In these circumstances it is easy to start sliding down a spiral path of depression and before you know it the momentum has reached such a pace that it is difficult to stop – a bit like a helter-skelter but with no end in sight. This is not the sort of situation you can 'pull yourself together' to get out of – professional help must be sought.

If, however, you do just feel a bit out of sorts, what is often called for is a boost. Chocolate does it for me, but it has to be a dark chocolate with at least 70 per cent cocoa solids for it to have any effect. I used to think it was psychological, but research has shown that chocolate contains two chemicals (anandamide and phenylethylamine) which do actually stimulate the brain and nervous system and promote feelings of well-being. But before you reach for the bar of high-sugar, milk chocolate, be warned: it has to be the dark variety – the darker the better.

You can also make a tisane (see page 190) with *Rosmarinus officinalis* (rosemary), *Melissa officinalis* (lemon balm), or *Mentha* x *piperata* (peppermint). Stir in a teaspoon of energy-giving honey whilst the tisane is still warm.

Alternatively, you can make some honey and oat bars which are packed with energising ingredients.

For 8 bars you will need:
300g rolled oats
100g chopped hazelnuts
100g chopped almonds
100g chopped walnuts

50g dried fruit – I like apple and raisin but the choice
is yours
½ teaspoon ground cinnamon
½ teaspoon rosemary leaves, pounded in a pestle and
mortar
175g honey – local if possible
125g unsalted butter

Pre-heat the oven to 180°C, 350°F, Gas mark 4.
Combine all the dry ingredients in a bowl. Put the honey
and butter in a saucepan and heat gently until the butter
has melted. Pour the honey and butter on to the dry
ingredients and mix thoroughly. Press the mixture into
a shallow tray and bake for about 25 minutes. Remove
from the oven and, whilst still warm and soft, mark out
the bars into squares, but do not remove from the tray.
Allow the mixture to cool and then re-cut the squares
and remove from the tray.

BITES AND STINGS

Being stung or bitten can cause an allergic reaction in some
people. If your tongue swells, you have difficulty breathing,
or you break out in a rash, you must seek medical attention
immediately – time is of the essence.

With any bite or sting you want instant relief! Herbal help
is usually close at hand. Rub a sprig of *Lavandula angustifolia*
(lavender) flowers between your fingers to release the essential
oil and then carefully rub it on the bite or sting. The juice from

*Plantago major* (plantain) leaves is also a good alleviator, as is *Aloe vera* gel. All of these will help with the pain.

If you have been stung by a bee you should first try to extract the sting. If you pinch it to try to pull it out you will merely inject more venom; instead you should scrape the sting out: I use the edge of a credit card but anything similar will do the trick. This won't work on wasp stings, of course, because they have the ability to sting more than once and therefore there is no physical sting to extract.

Received wisdom advocates the use of sodium bicarbonate on bee stings and ant bites, to neutralise their acid venom, but vinegar on wasp stings because their venom is alkaline. Whether the effect of the tiny amount of venom that has already been injected can be deactivated by a surface application of either vinegar or sodium bicarbonate is debateable but by all means try it – it won't do any harm.

BRUISING

Perhaps the most effective herb for bruising is *Arnica montana* (arnica), and arnica cream or ointment is readily available at chemists. I would advise against trying to grow your own arnica – it's a sub-alpine plant and would struggle with our wet winters. More importantly, however, it is subject to legal restrictions in some countries.

As well as helping to heal broken bones, a compress of *Symphytum officinale* (comfrey) is good for bruises and sprains.

BURNS AND SCALDS – INCLUDING SUNBURN

Only treat minor burns at home – as with any other injury, seek medical attention if the burn is severe.

There is one herb which stands out above all others for the treatment of minor burns – *Aloe vera*. The gel-like substance that is contained within its leaves is exceptional at easing the pain and promoting healing. With any burn or scald the first thing to do is to immerse the affected area in cold water – this should be done as soon as possible. Meanwhile you can cut a leaf off your *Aloe vera* plant; I keep mine on the kitchen windowsill – very handy for minor oven burns! Squeeze out some gel and apply it directly to the burn – don't worry about drying the area first because you may do more harm than good. Under no circumstances burst any blisters that may form; doing so is the quickest way for any infection to enter the now open wound.

You can also make some 'red oil' – olive oil infused with *Hypericum perforatum* (St John's wort) (see page 138). This is invaluable to use on burns, cuts, grazes and insect bites – a good all-rounder, in fact.

A cold compress (see page 189) made with *Fragaria vesca* (strawberry) leaves provides a soothing application to ease the symptoms of sunburn.

COLDS

It is claimed that some herbs, notably raw garlic, can help protect against catching a cold. Quite whether you would want to reek permanently of *Allium sativum* (garlic) is quite another matter, though! Some people also swear by *Echinacea* species (coneflower), although I am inclined to take the view that, with colds, you are either destined to get one or not. If you are unlucky enough to catch a cold, there is little that will actually cure it, but the symptoms can be relieved by taking a soothing tisane or, for a head cold, eased with a steam inhalation.

It almost goes without saying that if you develop symptoms other than those that you would expect from a 'normal' cold – like difficulty breathing or excessive headaches for example – you should consult your doctor immediately.

But for a 'normal' cold you can make a tisane (see page 190) from 3 teaspoons of fresh, or 2 teaspoons of dried leaves of *Mentha* x *piperata* (peppermint) and *Achillea millefolium* (yarrow), the same amount of *Echinacea* (coneflower) root, and a crushed clove of *Allium sativum* (garlic). Drink a cupful twice a day.

There is also much to be said in favour of the traditional alleviant of honey and lemon. Make a tisane with sliced lemon and add a teaspoon of honey. For a bit more zing, include a thin slice of *Zingiber officinale* (ginger) root.

If you have a head cold or are suffering from catarrh, a steam inhalation made with equal quantities (about 2 teaspoons) of *Thymus vulgaris* (thyme) leaves and *Mentha* x *piperata* (peppermint) leaves infused in 1 litre of boiling water will help. Allow the herbs to infuse for about 15 minutes then strain the liquid into a bowl. Cover your head with a towel and breathe in the steam.

I was given the following recipe by a friend of mine who, at the first sign of a sniffle, has a bowl of this flavourful soup and carries on having a portion every day until the cold gremlins pack their spotty hankies and search for pastures new. If you are not a chilli-lover you can reduce the amount, but as it is very beneficial I would advise you to include a small amount. He calls this soup his 'cold-combating cauldron'.

You will need:
1 tablespoon olive oil
1 small butternut squash, peeled, de-seeded and chopped into chunks
1 red onion, peeled and chopped
2 green chillies, de-seeded and chopped
4 cloves garlic, peeled and chopped
5cm piece of root ginger, peeled and chopped
100g shiitake mushrooms, sliced
Leaves from 1 sprig of thyme
1 litre vegetable stock

Heat the oil in a saucepan and add all the ingredients except the mushrooms, thyme and stock. Sauté them until the onion starts to soften. Add the mushrooms and thyme along with the stock and bring to the boil. Cover and simmer for about 20 minutes until the squash is very soft.

Take off the heat and blend until smooth.

CONSTIPATION

If you suffer from chronic constipation you should seek professional medical help. And if you eat a healthy, balanced diet with adequate fibre, constipation shouldn't be a problem. However, there may be an odd occasion when your bowels need a little assistance. One of the most pleasant tasting and effective, yet mild, laxatives is *Glycyrrhiza glabra* (liquorice) root. You can either just chew on the dried root or you can make a tisane of 1 teaspoon of root in a cup of water. Take this once or twice a day, but if the symptoms persist you must seek professional advice.

Alternatively, you can make a yogurt-based smoothie with laxative ingredients, which will help things along.

You will need:
250ml live yogurt
2 teaspoons flax seeds
2 thin slices of fresh *Zingiber officinale* (ginger)
2 teaspoons fresh *Mentha* x *piperata* (peppermint) leaves
2 teaspoons fresh *Petroselinum crispum* (parsley)

Pop everything into a blender and whizz the whole lot together – then drink!

COUGHS

Chronic coughs or prolonged bouts of coughing need medical intervention but for the occasional tickle a soothing, honey-based drink is comforting.

Honey has antibacterial and expectorant properties – and this is true of any honey, not just the highly-prized manuka honey. Add some herbs to aid decongestion and you have a treatment that not only eases your cough but tastes good too!

Take equal quantities of *Ocimum tenuiflorum* (holy basil), *Thymus vulgaris* (thyme) and *Origanum vulgare* (oregano) – about a tablespoon in all – and add them to a 250g jar of runny honey. Replace the lid and leave the mixture for about four weeks, turning upside down occasionally to distribute the herbs. Strain the honey through a sieve into a clean jar and store in a cool place.

Don't worry if your honey starts to set – all honey will set eventually. The length of time it takes depends on the glucose content of the nectar that the bees fed on.

Dissolve a teaspoon of the flavoured honey in a cup of hot water and sip. As with any herbal tea or tisane, you should not have any more than four cups a day, otherwise we are into the realms of medicinal doses which require professional guidance.

If you prefer to soothe your cough with a syrup here is a pleasant tasting one, full of herbs that will help ease the symptoms.

You will need:
25g of each of:
*Hyssopus officinalis* (hyssop) leaves
*Althaea officinalis* (marshmallow) root
*Glycyrrhiza glabra* (liquorice) root
*Verbascum thrapsus* (mullein) root

*Pimpinella anisum* (aniseed)
2 cinnamon sticks
1 litre water
About 1kg sugar

Place all the herbs except the hyssop into a pan and cover with the water. Bring to the boil and then simmer gently for about 20 minutes. Turn off the heat and add the hyssop. Allow the ingredients to infuse for a further 15 minutes. Strain the mixture into a measuring jug, taking note of how much liquid there is. Return the liquid to the pan and add the same amount in grammes of sugar as you have millilitres of liquid – so if you have 850ml liquid, add 850g sugar.

Heat the mixture, stirring continually until the sugar has dissolved, and then remove from the heat. Allow the syrup to cool and then pour into sterilised bottles (see page 192).

You can have a tablespoonful of this mixture up to six times a day

CUTS AND GRAZES

You really have to apply common sense when it comes to deciding at what point a cut becomes a wound. Home remedies should only be used on minor cuts and grazes – the ones that your own judgement tells you don't require a doctor's attention.

- *Calendula officinalis* (pot marigold) is one of the must-have herbs in your garden when it comes to first-aid. The flowers will help to stem bleeding, promote healing and prevent infection. Any cut or graze should be cleaned first and then you can carefully apply a salve containing marigold. Although marigold on its own is very effective, I have found that a combination of *Calendula officinalis* (pot marigold), *Plantago major* (plantain) and *Lavandula angustifolia* (lavender) works wonderfully. A simple salve can be made using the decoction method (see page 190) with coconut oil as a base.

- *Achillea millefolium* (yarrow) is also an effective herb to staunch the flow of blood: make a compress (see page 189) with yarrow and apply it to the wound.

- *Stachys officinalis* (woundwort), used in the same way, is good for cuts and grazes, too, especially if they show signs of becoming infected.

- An ointment or salve containing *Symphytum officinale* (comfrey) is also good for cuts and grazes.

DIARRHOEA

A 'dodgy tummy', as my Mum used to call a mild dose of diarrhoea, makes you feel wretched. Whenever I have a dodgy tummy, I find the easiest and most straightforward way of dealing with it is to not eat anything and drink only water for twenty-four hours. By this time I find the symptoms have disappeared and I allow myself some plain, boiled rice to break my fast. I picked up this tip from a midwife friend of mine, who pointed out that when babies are first weaned, they are given small quantities of rice to accustom their stomachs to solids – what better food for delicate adult stomachs, too.

A tisane made with *Fragaria vesca* (strawberry) leaves will also help, but if you find that your dodgy tummy is actually a raging gut, seek medical advice.

DIGESTION

Herbs have long played a part in helping with digestion. The fact that we have traditional pairings such *Mentha spicata* (mint) with lamb, *Foeniculum vulgare* (fennel) with oily fish and *Salvia officinalis* (sage) with pork is testament to this. Although there is no doubt that the herbs make the dish taste good, they also stimulate the digestive juices so that the fatty components of the food can be broken down more easily.

If you suffer from an occasional bout of indigestion, an infusion made from *Mentha* x *piperata* (peppermint) *or Fragaria vesca* (strawberry) leaves will help, as will *Pimpinella anisum* (aniseed). Obviously, if you have chronic indigestion or severe pain you should consult a doctor.

It's so easy to over-indulge, especially if you go out for a meal, or at special occasions like Christmas. It seemed a good idea at the time to finish off that last piece of cheesecake, beckoning temptingly from the plate, and just one more mince pie won't hurt! But the next day you really wished you hadn't. Here's a refreshing, tasty salad, full of zing, that might be just what your digestive system is crying out for following the previous day's onslaught.

You will need:
1 fennel bulb, finely sliced
1 small, cooked beetroot, sliced into matchsticks
1 large handful of rocket
Leaves from 5 or 6 sprigs of spearmint, torn into small pieces
Scant tablespoon of dressing made with olive oil and apple cider vinegar

Simply mix everything together. That's it!

ECZEMA

Like many problems with the skin, eczema is often the outward manifestation of an inner difficulty. It can be the result of an allergy or is indicative of stress or anxiety. These root causes have to be addressed professionally, of course, but in the meantime you can apply a soothing cream to help relieve the symptoms.

To make the cream, use the same method for making an oil decoction (see page 190) with coconut oil as the base. You can use *Calendula officinalis* (pot marigold) petals, *Chamaemelum nobile* (Roman chamomile) flowers and *Lavandula angustifolia* (lavender) flowers in equal quantities.

EYES

Eyes are delicate parts of our anatomy and should be managed with extreme caution. I am disinclined to use anything but a topical relief on my eyes. Some people are happy to use a home-made eyebath solution, but I am wary because the slightest contamination can spell disaster. Instead I like to use a cold compress (see page 189), which I apply to closed eyes. I use *Calendula officinalis* (pot marigold) petals in my compress, which is very soothing for tired or puffy eyes.

FLATULENCE

Flatulence can be embarrassing, but we really shouldn't be uneasy about it – it's a natural, bodily process after all, and we all suffer from it at some point or another. Excess wind can be relieved, however, by taking an infusion made with *Mentha spicata* (spearmint) and *Satureja montana* (winter savory) leaves and crushed *Anethum graveolens* (dill) seeds. Stirring in a little honey will make the tisane even tastier!

HANGOVER

If you have imbibed a little too much alcohol and have a hangover, the little imp on one of my shoulders is urging me to say, tough, you've only got yourself to blame! The more benevolent fairy on the other shoulder is suggesting that you take a tisane of *Achillea millefolium* (yarrow) and *Sambucus nigra* (elder) flowers to help your body get rid of the toxins!

**HAY FEVER**

Life can be pretty miserable for those among us who suffer from hay fever every year. It is estimated that one in five people are affected by it at some point during their lives, which is a pretty high percentage. Hay fever is an allergic reaction to plant pollen and can cause distress at different times of year, depending on what pollen is being released at the time. The only way to be completely free from hay fever is to avoid contact with pollen, which, unsurprisingly, is impossible to do during everyday life. Although hay fever can't be cured, the symptoms can be lessened.

Some people maintain that by taking a teaspoon of pollen-enriched honey each day, a certain amount of immunity can be built up. This will only be effective, though, if you can get honey from bees that have been foraging in your local region. The idea is that by ingesting some of the pollen that triggers the hay fever, a resistance to that pollen can be developed, in much the same way as homeopathic medicine is said to work.

You could also try tisanes made from *Hyssopus officinalis* (hyssop) or *Verbascum thrapsus* (mullein) – but separately, not all at once!

**HEADACHES AND MIGRAINE**

*Headaches*

A headache can be caused by any of a number of triggers and is often the manifestation of another concern. Stress can be a factor, or poor posture, or even constipation, and it is often difficult to pinpoint the reason for a headache. If you suffer from frequent or severe headaches you need to seek professional advice, but the occasional niggle can be helped by some herbal relief.

Tension headaches can be eased by placing a warm compress (see page 189) made with *Lavandula angustifolia* (lavender) on the forehead. You can replace the lavender with *Mentha* x *piperata* (peppermint): this too will alleviate the symptoms, as will *Tanacetum parthenium* (feverfew).

## *Migraine*

Migraine can hardly be described as a niggling annoyance – it can be totally debilitating. Apparently *Tanacetum parthenium* (feverfew) has been used in the treatment of migraine-type headaches since the first century CE. Its efficacy has been assessed in recent, fairly small-scale studies, although, because of the number of participants, the results were not conclusive. Nevertheless, a number of migraine sufferers continue to report that the symptoms ease when they take feverfew in a tisane (see page 190). As always, self-medication should be approached with caution, however, and if you do suffer regularly from migraines, you should consult your doctor.

## INSOMNIA

A sleepless night can really make you feel as if you have got out of the wrong side of the bed. Joking apart, lack of sleep is really not good for short- or long-term health. Although it is not advisable to rely on drugs, including natural ones, to help you sleep, there are times when an aid to relaxation is welcome and could be all that is needed.

One herb that has been used for generations to help you nod off is *Valeriana officinalis* (valerian). A tisane made with 2 to 3 grammes of dried rhizome, drunk an hour before bedtime will encourage sleep. If, however, you experience vivid dreams, or taking valerian actually makes your insomnia worse, you should stop taking it immediately.

A cup of *Chamaemelum nobile* (Roman chamomile) tisane will help too.

MEMORY

I'm assuming you are reading this entry because you have trouble remembering things not because you have a good memory! I am certain that as you get older forgetting things comes with the territory, but that doesn't mean that comprehensive memory loss is inevitable. There are some herbs that help with brain activity and there are suggestions that others can help reduce memory loss. Try an infusion (see page 190) of *Rosmarinus officinalis* (rosemary), *Thymus vulgaris* (thyme) and *Salvia officinalis* (sage) – 30g of each to 500ml of water is about right, if I remember correctly!

MUSCLES, ACHING

See Aching muscles

RASH

Much depends on the cause of the rash as to whether you can treat it yourself. Many rashes are symptomatic of another ailment, such as shingles, and you should seek medical advice.

Other rashes, however, may be due to something as simple as a nettle sting, in which case the following lotion will bring some relief.

You will need:
10g *Althaea officinalis* (marshmallow) root, chopped
10g *Chamaemelum nobile* (Roman chamomile) or *Matricaria recutita* (German chamomile) flowers
1 litre of water

Put the marshmallow root in a pan with the water and bring to a simmer. Heat for 5 minutes and then take the pan off the heat. Add the chamomile flowers and allow the mixture to infuse for 30 minutes or so until it is cool. Strain the liquid into a bottle. Soak a cotton wool pad in the liquid and apply to the rash as and when required.

SCALDS

See Burns and scalds

SORE THROAT

An age-old remedy for a sore throat, and still to my mind the best, is gargling with an infusion of *Salvia officinalis* (sage) leaves. The addition of a pinch of salt, some honey and some cider vinegar will further enhance the antiviral and antibacterial qualities of the gargle.

Make an infusion with 4 teaspoons fresh *Salvia officinalis* (sage) leaves and 200ml boiling water. After 15 minutes, add a pinch of salt, and 1 tablespoon each of honey and cider vinegar. Allow the mixture to cool and gargle with it up to six times a day.

SUNBURN

See Burns and scalds

TOOTHACHE

Toothache cannot be ignored: it is, almost without exception, the manifestation of a much deeper problem and you should seek out a dentist as soon as you can. Meanwhile you can apply a drop of oil of cloves, which will go some way to easing the pain.

TRAVEL SICKNESS

There is nothing guaranteed to spoil a holiday more than travel sickness. It's miserable. Help is at hand, though, in the form of *Zingiber officinale* (ginger). The most pleasant way of getting a dose to help with a queasy tummy is to suck on a piece of crystallised ginger: this is readily available, even in supermarkets, so you don't even have to go to the trouble of preserving it yourself. You can also make a tisane (see page 190) with a few slices of fresh ginger. Add a little honey if you find it unpalatable. Keep a flask of the tisane with you on your travels and sip it occasionally to keep the nausea at bay.

You can also make some ginger and chamomile biscuits to nibble on.

To make about 15 biscuits you will need:
100g butter
50g caster sugar
175g self-raising flour
1 teaspoon ground ginger
1 teaspoon dried chamomile flowers, pounded to a powder in a pestle and mortar

Cream the butter and sugar together until light. Add the flour, ground ginger and chamomile flowers to the mixture and lightly knead until it forms a dough. Then carefully roll out the dough on a lightly floured board until it is about 3mm thick before cutting into rounds using a 7.5cm cutter.

Arrange the biscuits on a lightly greased baking sheet and bake for about 30 minutes at 150°C, gas mark 2, or until the biscuits are a pale golden brown colour.

Cool on a wire rack and store in an airtight container.

## CHAPTER 4

# Cosmetic Herbs

Each year we spend millions of pounds trying to make our skin look clearer, our hands smoother and our hair more healthy. And each year we daub ourselves with no end of chemicals, trying to achieve those ends. And yet before the middle of the nineteenth century there were no commercially available cosmetics (unless you count soap). It took a certain Theron Tildon Pond to come up with his skin cream, 'Pond's Extract', also known as 'Pond's Golden Treasure', and in 1842, in America, the industrial cosmetics revolution was underway.

I don't want to give the impression that commercially produced preparations are in any way bad – they undergo stringent tests to make sure they are safe to use before they are allowed on the open market. Many people find, however, that some of the synthetically produced fragrances, colourings and preservatives that are used in the production of various cosmetics do not suit them and have started to look for those containing natural ingredients. It's a small step from that to actually making your own.

Of course the one major advantage of making your own preparations is that you know exactly what is in them, and therefore what is going on your skin. You should still be cautious, even when using natural ingredients, since some people may have an allergic reaction to certain plant constituents. Always rub a tiny amount on to your wrist and leave it for at least a day to check whether you have any adverse reactions.

Home-made cosmetics don't contain the same preservatives as commercially produced ones, it's true, and they may not have the same shelf life, but when you find out how simple it is to make your own, this is a minor concern.

As with many of the cleaning preparations that I look at in Chapter 5, it is often the base ingredients, rather than the herbs added to them, that do the 'work'. I am certain, however, that the herbal additions either make the products more effective, or, at the very least, make them smell nice!

# Face

The mantra for a lovely complexion has always been 'cleanse, tone, moisturise' and for many of my teenage years I couldn't quite understand why my complexion wasn't exactly 'lovely'. In fact, for much of the time, with a face full of freckles combined with spots, I turned back to soap and water, which didn't help in the slightest! But at last, when my teenage hormones had settled down a bit, I instigated the 'c-t-m' regime and have stuck with it ever since. I'm not claiming that I have film-star skin but it is skin that I can quite happily live with.

I haven't always made my own facial preparations but nowadays I find the practice therapeutic as well as good for my skin – and purse!


**CLEANSER**

One of the easiest cleansers to make has buttermilk as its base: in fact it has just three ingredients: 150ml buttermilk (readily available from supermarkets), 2 tablespoons of lemon juice, and 3 tablespoons of a herbal infusion of your choice. You simply whisk the whole lot together, pour it into a jar and keep it in the refrigerator. It will keep for up to a week.

You can alter the herbal infusion depending on your skin type.

- For normal skin try *Calendula officinalis* (pot marigold) petals, *Chamaemelum nobile* (Roman chamomile) flowers,

*Lavandula angustifolia* (lavender) flowers or *Rosa gallica* var. *officinalis* (Apothecary's rose) petals.

- If you have dry skin, you might find that *Calendula officinalis* (pot marigold) flowers, *Chamaemelum nobile* (Roman chamomile) flowers, *Sambucus nigra* (elder) flowers, or *Symphytum officinale* (comfrey) leaves are good choices.

- Oily skin would benefit from *Foeniculum vulgare* (fennel) leaves, *Salvia officinalis* (sage) leaves, *Rosmarinus officinalis* (rosemary) leaves, *Hamamelis virginiana* (witch hazel) bark or *Achillea millefolium* (yarrow) flowers and leaves.

- And if your skin is sensitive, try *Calendula officinalis* (pot marigold) petals, *Chamaemelum nobile* (Roman chamomile) flowers, or *Althaea officinalis* (marshmallow) root.

To use the cleanser, simply soak a cotton wool pad in the milk and wipe it gently over your face and neck, avoiding the eye area. That's it!

**TONER**

A toner with a pedigree must surely be Queen of Hungary Water, dating back to the 1300s. Apparently, like the original *Kölnisch Wasser* (4711 Eau de Cologne), it was initially made to be a tonic, to be drunk. Only subsequently was it used externally as a perfume, an addition to bathing water, or as a skin toner. The exact ingredients and their proportions have been lost over the years but it seems the consensus is that vinegar, and more specifically cider vinegar, was the base.

To make a modern-day version, take equal quantities of the leaves of *Melissa officinalis* (lemon balm), *Rosmarinus officinalis* (rosemary) and *Salvia officinalis* (sage); the flowers of *Sambucus nigra* (elder), *Calendula officinalis* (pot marigold) and *Chamaemelum nobile* (Roman chamomile) or *Matricaria recutita* (German chamomile); and the petals of *Rosa gallica* var. *officinalis* (Apothecary's rose). Put them in a jar and cover them with enough cider vinegar to ensure that all the herbs are immersed. Pop on the lid and leave the mixture for two weeks. Strain it and dilute the liquid with distilled water at a ratio of 2 parts infused vinegar to 1 part water.

## MOISTURISER

Once you have cleansed and toned your skin it's a good idea to moisturise. Moisturising won't stop the skin ageing or keep wrinkles entirely at bay but it will help to keep the skin hydrated.

A friend of mine swears by using a scant application of a decoction (see page 190) of coconut oil and *Rosa gallica* var. *officinalis* (Apothecary's rose) petals and I have to say she does have lovely skin. I tried it and found it a little too oily – and my dog kept licking me! So I found this recipe, which works well for my normal, but mature, skin!

You will need:
1 teaspoon of beeswax

1 teaspoon of shea butter (or lanolin if you prefer)

1 tablespoon of almond oil

3 tablespoons of *Rosa gallica* var. *officinalis* (Apothecary's rose) petal infusion (see page 190)

4 or 5 drops of rose essential oil (optional). Be sure to use essential oil, which contains only natural oil, and not fragrance oil, which is usually a synthetic product.

Melt the beeswax and shea butter together in a double saucepan. When they have melted take the pan off the heat. Meanwhile, gently warm the almond oil and then stir it into the melted wax and butter. Warm the rose petal infusion and gradually beat it into the wax, butter and oil mixture, drop by drop, until you have the desired consistency and the mixture is cold. If you want a little more fragrance, you can add four or five drops of rose essential oil as the mixture cools. Spoon the cream into sterilised jars (see page 192) and don't forget to label them.

If you have a different skin type you can substitute the rose petal infusion with one suggested for cleansers, above.

SCRUB

Every now and then your face needs to be exfoliated to get rid of any dead skin cells that are not removed during normal cleansing. A gentle but effective scrub is required and one containing finely ground oats and rice flour fits the bill perfectly. The following scrub is suitable for all skin types.

You will need:

2 tablespoons of finely ground oatmeal

1 tablespoon of rice flour

1 teaspoon dried *Calendula officinalis* (pot marigold) petals

1 teaspoon dried *Rosa gallica* var. *officinalis* (Apothecary's rose) petals

½ teaspoon *Daucus carota* (carrot) seeds

Plain yogurt

Grind the calendula petals, rose petals and carrot seeds to a fine powder in a pestle and mortar. Put them in a bowl with the oatmeal and rice flour and mix them together well. Add enough yogurt to make a paste and gently massage it into damp skin. Finally, rinse off with clean water.

MASK OR PACK

There's nothing quite like a soak in the bath. Add a moisturising face pack and it's even more relaxing. Add a glass of bubbly and you are in heaven! I can't promise you heaven but this face pack hits the spot as far as relaxation goes because for the best results you need to leave it on for 15 minutes.

You will need:

Half an avocado pear, peeled, stoned and mashed or, if you have sensitive skin, use half an ordinary pear, peeled and grated

1 tablespoon of honey
1 tablespoon double cream
Rice flour

Simply mix the pear, honey and cream together in a
bowl and add enough rice flour to make a paste. Smooth
it over the skin, avoiding the sensitive eye area and lie
back! Rinse it off with lukewarm water.

# Hands

Hands are one part of your body that really take a battering
so they more than anything will appreciate some pampering.

There are really two kinds of preparation that will benefit
your hands – a barrier cream and a moisturising cream.

**BARRIER CREAM**

This does what it says on the tin: it forms a barrier between
the skin and the environment so that moisture is trapped in
and other substances are kept away from the skin. It should
be applied to completely dry skin before you do any work.
To be effective the cream obviously has to contain some
sort of waterproofing agent. One of the most successful is
petroleum jelly. Take four tablespoons of petroleum jelly and
melt in a double saucepan or a bowl over simmering water.
Add as many *Lavandula angustifolia* (lavender) flowers and

*Chamaemelum nobile* (Roman chamomile) or *Matricaria recutita* (German chamomile) flowers as the melted jelly can take, and heat gently for about 45 minutes. Take the pan off the heat and strain it through a fine mesh sieve into pots. Allow the mixture to cool and then pop on the lids.

Some people are averse to using petroleum jelly so an alternative is at hand. Take two tablespoons of beeswax – 'pelleted' beeswax is ideal. Melt it gently in a double saucepan and gradually stir in 10 tablespoons of olive oil. When all the oil has been incorporated pour the mixture into pots and cover them when the cream is cool.

You can use other oils apart from olive oil if you wish – almond oil is lovely but much more expensive of course. Or you could use an infused oil. Oil infused with *Chamaemelum nobile* (Roman chamomile) or *Matricaria recutita* (German chamomile), *Lavandula angustifolia* (lavender) or *Sambucus nigra* (elder) flowers is ideal.

MOISTURISING CREAM

This type of cream is used to replace moisture that has been lost through everyday activity, so it needs to be able to penetrate the epidermis rather than form a barrier and is therefore applied after you have washed your hands.

Here is a basic recipe which gives you some leeway as to the particular ingredients you use. It's very similar to the recipe for the face cream, above, but with slightly different proportions.

It consists of just four ingredients: a solid oil, a liquid oil, an emulsifier and water.

Suitable solid oils, which are hard at room temperature but melt at body temperature are: lard, coconut oil, cocoa butter, and lanolin.

Liquid oils include olive, sunflower, almond, and jojoba. These could be infused with a herb such as *Lavandula angustifolia* (lavender) or *Calendula officinalis* (pot marigold), if you wish.

Beeswax is the best emulsifier, and use ordinary, distilled water.

You will need 3 parts of solid oil, 6 parts of the liquid oil, 1 part of emulsifier and 9 parts of water. You can use any amount you choose, as long as you stick to the correct proportions. So for example, if you have three tablespoons of solid oil, you would use six tablespoons of liquid oil and so on.

Melt the solid oil in a double saucepan or bowl over simmering water and then add the liquid oil. Now incorporate the beeswax, either in pelleted form, or from a block which has been grated.

While the beeswax is melting, heat the water so that it is slightly warmer than body temperature.

When the beeswax has melted, take the pan off the heat and let the mixture cool to the same temperature as the water. Very gradually whisk in the water – use a balloon whisk or an electric hand whisk to do this. The mixture will go thick and creamy. As soon as all the water has been incorporated spoon the mixture into sterilised jars (see page 192).

As well as being a really good hand cream this is also suitable for the rest of your body.

# Hair

**SHAMPOO**

The next time you're in the supermarket or chemist, have a look at just how many shampoos contain herbs or herb extracts. I think you'll be amazed. And it goes to show that using herbs in hair care products is as popular now as it has always been.

The purpose of shampoo is, of course, to clean the hair. To do this there has to be some kind of soap or soap-like medium which acts as a dirt-holding agent. Before the advent of what we recognise as soap there was one herb which stood out as being the main source of saponin, the chemical that does the cleaning. This herb was, and still is, *Saponaria officinalis*, otherwise known as soapwort. It still makes an effective cleaner and, combined with *Equisetum arvense* (horsetail), it has conditioning properties too.

To make a gentle shampoo you will need:
8 tablespoons of *Equisetum arvense* (horsetail) stems, snipped into pieces and slightly bruised
8 tablespoons of *Saponaria officinalis* (soapwort) root, grated and soaked overnight
2 litres of distilled water

Drain the soapwort root and put it, together with the horsetail, in a pan. Add the water and bring to the boil. Simmer for 15 minutes and then take the pan off the heat and allow the mixture to infuse for about an hour.

Strain the infusion into bottles. You need to be generous with the amount you use when washing your hair – about 300ml is needed. Be careful to keep the shampoo away from your eyes, though – the soapwort can cause irritation.

You can also use home-made soap on your hair. You may think this would be much too harsh to use as a shampoo but it is much milder than many commercial products, and you can add particular herbs suited to your hair type. There is a recipe in the soap section, below.

HAIR RINSE

This can be used as a final rinse rather than just using water. All you need is 1 part apple cider vinegar to 2 parts boiling water and about five tablespoons in total of your chosen herbs.

To make the rinse, first make a decoction (see page 190) with the herbs and boiling water. Allow the herbs to steep until the water is cool. Strain the herbs and then add the vinegar to the liquid. That's it! The table below will give you some ideas of which herbs to use.

| Hair type | Herb |
|---|---|
| Normal | *Equisetum arvense* (horsetail), *Origanum majorana* (sweet marjoram), *Rosmarinus officinalis* (rosemary), *Thymus vulgaris* |

| Hair type | Herb |
|---|---|
| | (thyme), *Urtica dioica* (nettle), *Tropaeolum majus* (nasturtium) |
| Dry | *Sambucus nigra* (elder) flowers, *Althaea officinalis* (marshmallow) |
| Greasy | *Lavandula angustifolia* (lavender), *Mentha* x *piperata* (peppermint), *Rosmarinus officinalis* (rosemary) |
| Prone to dandruff | *Petroselinum crispum* (parsley), *Rosmarinus officinalis* (rosemary), *Urtica dioica* (nettle) |
| Dull | *Foeniculum vulgare* (fennel), *Petroselinum crispum* (parsley) |
| Fair | *Chamaemelum nobile* (Roman chamomile) or *Matricaria recutita* (German chamomile) flowers |
| Dark | *Salvia officinalis* (sage), *Thymus vulgaris* (thyme) |
| Auburn | *Calendula officinalis* (pot marigold) flowers |

# Bathing and Showering

I sometimes think that those cultures which advocate showering to get clean and then bathing to relax have got it right. We can't all do that but we can make showering or bathing an invigorating or relaxing experience, depending on what we feel like at the time.

SOAP

Whether we bathe or shower the one thing that we need to do is to clean ourselves and for that we need some kind of soap.

I love hand-made soap that is made by the cold process method – it is rich and creamy and quite unlike any 'ordinary' soap. You can make your own but it is very involved: if you do want to have a go there are a number of books that will help you. Although I have made my own soap from scratch, I now cheat a bit and buy a simple, unfragranced, cold processed soap made with olive oil and shea butter and add some extras of my own. It's very simple to do.

> You will need a 100g bar of soap, grated
> 1 teaspoon of clear honey
> 1 teaspoon of *Lavandula angustifolia* (lavender) flowers, ground to powder in a pestle and mortar – or any other herb you fancy – *Pelargonium capitatum* (rose-scented pelargonium) has a lovely fragrance.
> 2 to 3 drops of lavender or other essential oil (this is optional)
>
> To use as a shampoo, choose a herb to suit your hair type (see above).
>
> Melt the soap in a double saucepan or bowl over simmering water. Stir in the honey and powdered lavender until they are well blended and then take the pan off the heat. Allow it to cool a little and add

the essential oil if you are using it. While the mixture is still liquid, pour it into a mould – a small tin lined with baking parchment is ideal – and allow it to harden. Because of the addition of honey, this may well take several days.

Instead of pouring the soap into a mould you could also make individual washballs. Let the mixture cool a little more and then take teaspoonfuls of it and form them into little balls. Put them on a sheet of baking parchment and, again, allow them to harden.

HERBAL BATH SACHETS

One of the easiest ways of enjoying some fragrant herbs at bath time is to make small sachets of them out of butter muslin. Simply cut a square of muslin and pile some herb flowers or leaves in the centre. Gather up the muslin to form a little pouch and tie it with a long piece of string. You can then hang the pouch from the hot water tap. Don't be tempted to just fling a few flowers or petals into the bath – they will cling to your body as you get out of the bath and they are a dickens of a job to get off!

BATH BOMBS

Bath bombs are incredibly easy to make and certainly add a fizz to bath time!

The basic ingredients are sodium bicarbonate and citric

acid. You then add drops of whatever fragrant essential oil you like. I like to make a slightly different franced bomb every time but in general my two favourites are citrus, using essential oils of *Aloysia triphylla* (lemon verbena) and *Citrus sinensis* (orange) blossom, and what I call my Provençal fragrance, using essential oils of *Lavandula angustifolia* (lavender), *Rosmarinus officinalis* (rosemary) and *Thymus vulgaris* (thyme). Experiment a little until you find a combination you like.

Although dried petals and flowers make the bombs look really pretty, they will float around in your bath and are a nightmare to get off your skin at the end of your soak. They can also clog up the drain, so I avoid using them.

To make four small bombs you will need:
80g of sodium bicarbonate
1 tablespoon of citric acid
10 drops in total of your chosen essential oil(s)
A pinch of finely chopped dried petals or flowers, or very finely grated citrus peel (optional)

Simply mix the sodium bicarbonate and the citric acid together on a plate and sprinkle the essential oil(s) over it. Also sprinkle on any petals or other ingredients you may like to include. Now gather the mixture together and either form it into four small balls or press it into moulds such as ice-cube trays. Store the bath bombs in a dry place and use within two months.

If you want to give the bath bombs as a present you can wrap them first in aluminium foil and then in pretty tissue paper and finish off the package with a ribbon.

## BODY SCRUB

Like your face, your body will appreciate an exfoliating session now and again. This recipe contains ingredients that are a little coarser than the face scrub because your body skin can cope with a little more abrasion. Please don't think this body scrub is like sandpaper, though! It contains lots of other lovely ingredients to truly pamper your skin.

> You will need:
> 2 tablespoons walnut kernels, finely ground
> 2 tablespoons of medium ground oatmeal
> 1 tablespoon of rice flour
> 2 tablespoons of honey
> 1 teaspoon dried *Chamaemelum nobile* (Roman chamomile) or *Matricaria recutita* (German chamomile) flowers
> 1 teaspoon dried *Thymus vulgaris* (thyme) leaves

Grind the chamomile flowers and thyme leaves to a fine powder in a pestle and mortar. Put them in a bowl with the walnuts, oatmeal and rice flour and mix them together well. Add the honey to make a paste. If the paste is too firm, add a little more honey.

This scrub is best used in the shower: dampen your skin and then gently massage in the scrub. Rinse off under the shower.

# Cologne

We all have our favourite perfumes. Sometimes, though, we may just want a suggestion of a fragrance, a waft of something refreshing or calming. This is where a herbal cologne can be just the ticket – and it is very simple to make.

You will need:

6 tablespoons in total of your chosen herb(s) – try *Melissa officinalis* (lemon balm) and *Aloysia triphylla* (lemon verbena) for a citrusy scent, or *Rosa gallica* var. *officinalis* (Apothecary's rose) petals and *Pelargonium capitatum* (rose-scented pelargonium), or straightforward *Lavandula angustifolia* (lavender)

300ml distilled water

6 tablespoons of vodka

Simply put all the ingredients into a screw-top jar. Leave the mixture to infuse for at least ten days, shaking it every day. Then strain the liquid through a sieve, pressing the herbs to extract the maximum fragrance. Pour the liquid into one or more bottles, cover and label. You should keep your cologne in a cool, dark place.

# Teeth

If you are bewildered by the number and variety of tooth-pastes available at your local chemist or supermarket, now might be the time to go back to basics. You can actually make your own perfectly effective toothpaste using a minimum of ingredients. For one teeth-cleaning session you will need:

> 1 teaspoon of bicarbonate of soda *or*
> ½ teaspoon of bicarbonate of soda and ½ teaspoon of powdered *Fragaria vesca* (strawberry) root
> 2 drops of essential oil of peppermint

Simply mix the ingredients together with enough water to make a paste, and there you have it!

MOUTHWASH

If you like to finish off your teeth cleaning with a mouthwash, here is a recipe with antiseptic and breath-sweetening properties.

*Thyme and Mint Mouthwash*
You will need:
500ml water
1 teaspoon fresh *Mentha spicata* (spearmint) leaves
1 teaspoon fresh *Thymus vulgaris* (thyme) leaves
1 teaspoon of *Pimpinella anisum* (aniseed)

Make an infusion (see page 190) with the ingredients. Allow it to cool then strain it and use as a mouthwash and gargle.

TEETH WHITENER

If you want to keep your teeth relatively stain-free here is a simple recipe using an unlikely ingredient.

Mash two or three *Fragaria vesca* strawberries (the little wild ones) to a pulp and spread the pulp on your teeth. Leave it there for five minutes or so and then rinse your mouth with water to which a scant half-teaspoon of bicarbonate of soda has been added. Do this once a week.

CHAPTER 5

# *Herbs in the Home*

This chapter deals with ways in which you can use herbs in the home. In what follows I am looking at a whole range of applications, except how to use the herbs in cooking: I have covered this latter aspect in another book, *The Kitchen Herb Garden*.

# Cleaning with Herbs

The chances are that if you are reading this book you are interested in, and care about, the environment in which we live. I wouldn't mind hazarding a guess, too, that you do your best to 'practise what you preach', perhaps by buying free-range eggs, supporting local businesses or recycling as much as possible.

One area that often slips under the radar, though, is the use of chemicals. We can't actually get away from using chemicals – even 'natural' products contain them – but we can perhaps be aware of using 'good' chemicals as opposed to those that may harm the environment. One easy way of doing this is by using eco-friendly cleaning products.

In some ways I am being a little disingenuous with the heading of this section. I have implied that you can clean with herbs whereas it is nearly always the base product that does the cleaning, and the herbs are often an added extra. Even so, here are a few general cleaning preparations making use of herbs which can be used throughout the home.

GENERAL PURPOSE CLEANERS

There is no doubt that one of the most effective natural cleaners is vinegar. Now I'm not suggesting you go around your home wiping surfaces with a cloth saturated in brown malt vinegar – your home would soon end up smelling like a fish and chip shop. But clear, distilled malt vinegar infused with herbs will do a sterling job of keeping just about every surface clean and fragrant. The exception is marble. Vinegar and marble just don't go together – the acidic nature of the vinegar will etch into the limestone of the marble to create pits and discolouring, so choose a cleaner specially formulated for your precious surface.

To make herb vinegar cleaning fluid, simply chop a couple of handfuls of herbs such as *Mentha spicata* (spearmint), *Rosmarinus officinalis* (rosemary), *Lavandula angustifolia* (lavender) or *Aloysia triphylla* (lemon verbena) and put them in a lidded jar. Pour 500ml distilled vinegar over the herbs, put the lid on, and leave to infuse for three or four days. Strain the vinegar into a plastic spray bottle and use as required. Although you can use the cleaner at full strength, I tend to dilute it 50/50 with water for everyday use.

If you don't want to use vinegar in your cleaning preparation there is an alternative in the form of borax, a naturally occurring, alkaline mineral. To make a borax cleaner, prepare some herbs as you would for the vinegar spray but instead of covering them with vinegar, steep them in 500ml water for a few days. Strain the water into a jug and stir in two tablespoons of borax until it has dissolved. Decant the mixture into a spray bottle and it's ready to use.

FURNITURE POLISH

I now have to come clean – excuse the pun – and admit my love of bees. Honey bees to be precise. Not only do they provide the vital pollination of plants; they also give us honey, and, more importantly for this part of the book, wax.

Beeswax has been used for centuries as the base for furniture polish and although you can buy such a polish from the supermarket it's very easy to make yourself. Add an infusion of herbs to the mixture and you have an effective and sweet-smelling polish.

To make about 600ml of polish you will need:
50g beeswax
300ml turpentine
50g vegetable-based soap, grated
200ml herb infusion (see page 190), such as *Lavandula angustifolia* (lavender), *Rosmarinus officinalis* (rosemary) or *Aloysia triphylla* (lemon verbena)

Grate the beeswax and put it, with the turpentine, into the top of a double saucepan or bowl over a pan of simmering water. (Turpentine is highly flammable, so always use an indirect heat source.) Heat until the ingredients are well blended, stirring continuously. Remove the pan from the heat and allow the beeswax mixture to cool slightly.

In a separate pan, gently heat the soap and herb infusion, whisking until the mixture is frothy. Remove the pan from the heat and allow the mixture to cool slightly.

Stir the soap mixture into the beeswax mixture to make a thick, creamy paste. Pour into a wide-topped container with a lid, and don't forget to label it! Use the polish sparingly and rub off with a soft cloth.

SCOURER

The bane of most gardeners' lives are those perennial weeds which, if once they have a foot-hold (or should it be root-hold) in their gardens are notoriously difficult to get rid of. Of course there are ways to be rid of them – eventually – unless they are *Equisetum arvense*, otherwise known as horsetail which, in my experience, will defy any attempt at eradication. This isn't surprising, since the root system can penetrate down to thirty feet and it has survived as a genus for about 300 million years.

Despite its bad press, horsetail does have a use. The coating of fine silica crystals on the surface of its aerial parts, which has enabled it to survive for so long, also makes it a first-rate scouring medium. So throw away the wire wool and sponges with an abrasive surface and gather a few stems of horsetail. Roll them into a ball and there you have it – a natural scouring pad!

MILD CLEANER

From one end of the cleaning scale to the other now. Some materials around the home require gentle cleaning and once again nature has provided us with a substance that will do the job. The common name of *Saponaria officinalis* (soapwort) is the give-away clue to its use. Long before commercial soaps became available, soapwort was used to clean all manner of things including the face, hair and fabrics. Even today, it is used by museums and other conservators to launder or clean delicate fabrics and tapestries, so if you have a treasured heirloom such as an embroidered cloth or some lacework, a soapwort 'shampoo' may be just what you need.

To make about a litre of 'shampoo' you will need:
25g dried *Saponaria officinalis* (soapwort) root, soaked overnight *or* 3 handfuls of fresh soapwort stems, flowers removed
1 litre of water – filtered rainwater is top notch; otherwise use distilled water (avoid tap water with its added chemicals if you can)

If you are using dried root, drain it, cut it into small pieces and bash it with a hammer or rolling pin. If you are using fresh stems, cut them into short lengths and bruise them slightly. This will allow the saponins – the 'active ingredient' which provides the cleaning action – to be released more readily.

Put the root or stem into a pan, add the water and bring to the boil. Turn the heat down and simmer gently for about 30 minutes, stirring occasionally. Remove the pan from the heat and allow the liquid to cool completely before removing the remains of the herbs and straining the liquid into a bottle. Label your bottle! You can use the 'shampoo' undiluted or dilute it with some distilled water if the fabric just needs freshening.

# Fragrances

### CLOTHES RINSE

Someone asked me the other day what luxury I would afford myself if money were no object. A posh new car? A worldwide cruise? Neither. I would like fresh, high quality, cotton bed linen every day for the rest of my life. Not new, but newly laundered – by someone else, of course! And I would like the final rinse to include an infusion of *Lavandula angustifolia* (lavender), or *Rosa gallica* var. *officinalis* (Apothecary's rose), depending on my mood!

Well, I know I will never have fresh bed linen *every* day, but when I do, I can have it rinsed in lavender or rose – this time doing it myself. At least this way I can pretend that money is no object! An infusion is very easy to make (see page 190) and can be used to rinse not only bed linen, but also fine linen and lingerie.

### POT POURRI

It's a shame that nowadays the term pot pourri often conjures up visions of dried out bits of non-descript, bark-like substances collecting dust in a bowl that some well-meaning friend gave you for your birthday about five years ago. Either that, or a bag of equally non-descript wood shavings, leaves and other 'botanicals' that the packet says will remind us of fluffy towels or Christmas cookies or will instantly transport us to a tropical paradise filled with the scent of vanilla, mango and ginger – all at once!

Harking back to days gone by isn't always a good idea but I think when it comes to pot pourri, it is worth more than a backward glance. Flowers have long been used to scent the home, but it was during the eighteenth century that the pot pourri came into its own. Pot pourri was originally a culinary term roughly meaning a pot of mixed vegetables (literally 'rotten' or 'addled' pot, from the French for 'rotten': *pourri, à la pourriture*), but it was somehow hijacked and came to mean a pot of mixed fragrant flowers, herbs and spices – far from rotten! Bowls of pot pourri would be strategically placed around the home to fragrance the air – there were no artificial room sprays back then!

Unlike the modern, mixtures, a traditional pot pourri always contains roses, with whatever other flowers, petals, leaves and spices are available or desired. A fixative is required, too, to prolong the fragrance: orris root powder, from *Iris germanica* var. *florentina*, is still widely used. And if you want a more intense scent, you can add a few drops of an essential oil.

### Dry pot pourri

The easiest type of pot pourri to make is a dry mixture. The ingredients are calculated by weight or volume, as we shall see in this basic herbal recipe.

You will need:
2 to 3 teaspoons of your chosen spice(s)
25g of powdered *Iris germanica* var. *florentina* (orris) root
6 drops of essential oil (optional)

1 litre in total of fragrant petals of your choice – this can
be one variety or a mixture
25g fragrant herb leaves
1 teaspoon of additional ingredients, such as cloves,
grated orange rind or star anise (optional)

To make the pot pourri, mix together the spices, orris
root and essential oil. If you use essential oil, rub the
mixture between your fingers and thumb to make sure
the oil is evenly distributed.

In a separate bowl, mix together the rest of the
ingredients. Add the spice mixture to the bowl and mix
thoroughly. Put the mixture into an airtight container
and store in a dark place for at least five weeks. Shake the
container occasionally to redistribute the ingredients.
After the 'maturing' time, put the pot pourri in a
decorative bowl, or use it to fill bags.

### *Moist pot pourri*
You can also make a moist pot pourri. The end result isn't
as visually attractive as the dry version but the fragrance
is more intense.

You will need exactly the same amount of ingredients
as the dry mixture, but in addition, you will need some
coarse salt, brown sugar and brandy.

You will not need the spices, orris root, essential oil,
or optional, additional ingredients until the second part
of the recipe.

Firstly you have to make the 'stock pot'. This uses the litre of fragrant petals and 25g of herbs. Mix these together in a bowl. Now take a jar with a tight-fitting lid and put in a layer of petals and herbs – about a centimetre is enough. Sprinkle this with some salt, just thickly enough to cover the petals. Add another layer of petals, followed by salt. Now take a pinch of brown sugar and scatter this over the salt, and then sprinkle a few drops of brandy on top. Carry on building up the layers in this sequence until you have used all the petals. Seal the jar and leave it for eight weeks to 'cure'. If a lot of liquid accumulates in this time, drain it off and re-seal the jar.

At the end of the curing time, the mixture will have formed into a cake-like substance. Now you can crumble this into the rest of the ingredients that you set aside. Put the entire mixture into an airtight container and let it mature for another two weeks. Because the mixture isn't as attractive as the dry pot pourri, you may like to put it into a bowl with a perforated lid, or, if you use an open bowl, arrange some dried flowers over the top.

You can concoct your own pot pourri mixes. One of my favourite mixes includes rose petals, rose buds, lemon verbena and lavender. Experiment a little until you find your own favourite.

TUSSIE MUSSIES OR NOSEGAYS

Quite where the name tussie mussie came from is lost in the annals of time, although there is a reference to it the *Promptorium Parvulorum*, a Latin word list dating from the 1440s. And you couldn't really guess what a tussie mussie actually is from its name. Nosegay is a little easier to explain: the nose bit is obvious; gay is apparently an archaic term for toy or ornament. So we have a toy for the nose! You are still no wiser? Well, let's call it by yet another alternative name – posy. That's better! We all know that a posy is made up of a variety of flowers and greenery and is like a 'mini' bouquet.

Traditionally, these posies were made up of the flowers and greenery of aromatic herbs, chosen either for their fragrance or their disinfectant properties, and this gives us a clue to why they were carried in the first place. When malodorous smells and infection were rife, both ladies and gentlemen would carry them under their noses (hence nosegay) to keep such smells and contagion at bay.

Many believed that diseases of all kinds were air-borne so these posies of herbs were the first line of defence, particularly during periods when the plague was prevalent. The posies would almost always contain herbs such as *Ruta graveoloens* (rue), *Artemisia abrotanum* (southernwood), *Rosmarinus officinalis* (rosemary), *Salvia officinalis* (sage) and *Thymus vulgaris* (thyme), all of which have antiseptic properties.

Later, during the Victorian era, when floriography (otherwise known as the language of flowers, where each flower carries with it a particular meaning, and sometimes more than one) was popular, the carrying and sending of tussie mussies took on an additional function. As well as being fragrant, they could also convey a message: for example, mint means virtue, a red rosebud signifies purity and loveliness, myrtle stands for love. Such tussie mussies are assembled in a particular way. There is a central flower, such as a rose, and then concentric circles of other herbs and flowers arranged around it. A decorative surround of leaves finishes off the posy, and the whole thing is tied together with ribbon, raffia or string.

The custom of making and giving tussie mussies seems to be undergoing a bit of a renaissance just now. And, if you grow your own herbs and flowers, how lovely it is to pick some to give to a friend for their birthday, or to celebrate the birth of a child, or even to express sympathy if there is a bereavement – to my mind, much nicer than shop-bought flowers.

To give you an idea, here is a 'recipe' for a birthday tussie mussie for a friend.

In the centre, a *Pelargonium capitatum* (rose-scented pelargonium), meaning preference, with a selection of the following surrounding it:

- *Valeriana officinalis* (valerian) flowers – accommodating disposition
- *Petroselinum crispum* (parsley) – festivity
- *Ocimum basilicum* (sweet basil) – good wishes
- *Fragaria vesca* (wild strawberry) – perfection
- *Mentha spicata* (spearmint) – warmth of sentiment

- A final circle of *Foeniculum vulgare* (fennel) meaning worthy of all praise; this would finish it off very nicely.

If you do give a tussie mussie, be sure to send a note of the meaning of the flowers. Some plants can have double, contradictory meanings; for example, *Lavandula angustifolia* (lavender) can mean constancy and devotion, but it can also mean distrust!

### WREATH

You could extend the floriography idea further and use different herbs in a festive wreath. We are used to seeing them hanging on our doors at Christmas time, but what about making one for other festive events, such as Easter, harvest, a birthday, or as a 'welcome home' gesture? And you don't even have to slavishly follow the language of flowers – any combination of herbs can be attractive.

I tend to use a wreath base made with florist's foam. The plant material will stay fresher for much longer and can be replaced if one herb gets past its best before the others.

### HERB TEA

Another idea, the result of which I gave to a friend of mine for her birthday, was a herb tea with a difference. Describing it as a herb tea is perhaps a little misleading because it was actually a very pretty cup and saucer (which she could use later) with a small selection of herbs arranged in florist's foam inside the cup. I used herbs that could be made into tisanes, such as *Mentha spicata* (spearmint) and *Aloysia triphylla* (lemon verbena), but I sent an explanatory note with it in case she decided to brew up everything at the same time!

## Pest Repellents

**FLIES**

I spent many years living in the country with a scarecrow in the garden, skylarks singing overhead, livery stables down the road, and beautiful Jersey cows munching their way through the meadow a stone's throw away. The perfect pastoral idyll? You would think so, yes. Except that where there are animals, there are flies. This is an inevitable and inescapable fact. Now, you can spray the disease-ridden bugs with a chemical concoction which, I have to say, is very effective but not exactly environmentally friendly.

You can put up sticky fly papers in the hope that they will fling themselves against them, in a final *kamikaze* act.

You can line up a windowsill full of *Dionaea muscipula* (Venus flytraps) and watch with malevolent glee as the creatures are slowly digested.

During the summer holidays a friend of mine armed her two children with fly swats and paid them a penny for each dead fly – it certainly kept them busy and reduced the fly population at the same time!

However, several years ago I was introduced to a less

drastic (and potentially less expensive!) method of dealing with the pesky creatures. There are a number of herbs which will naturally repel flies and other flying insects. The herbs won't kill them, of course, but by strategically placing vases of such herbs around the home, and particularly in the kitchen, you will go some way to keeping the bugs at bay – a first line of defence, as it were.

I first came across this idea when I visited the inspiring *Weald and Downland Open Air Museum*, near Chichester in West Sussex, home to a number of 'rescued' buildings which have been reconstructed as near to their original design as possible. Despite the midden, or waste heap, being fairly close to the Tudor house that we were looking at, there were surprisingly few flies buzzing around. When I asked about this, the guide said the herbs that were strewn on the floor, and those in the pots on the tables were natural fly deterrents – no aerosols back then!

Among the herbs used at the museum were *Lavandula angustifolia* (lavender), *Mentha spicata* (mint), *Rosmarinus officinalis* (rosemary), *Ruta graveoloens* (rue) and *Tanacetum vulgare* (tansy). All of these can be used fresh, or they can be dried and made into a pot pourri (see page 98).

Another centuries-old insect repellent is 'Vinegar of the Four Thieves'. Legend has it that when the plague was raging in the town of Toulouse, the looting of homes in which the inhabitants had died was rife. Four such looters, despite their risky occupation, seemed to remain untouched by the plague. Eventually they were caught and, instead of being executed, they struck a deal with the judge by offering him their secret plague-resistant recipe. Such a tale is plausible, since the ingredients are herbs which are insect repellents. We may not be plagued by the plague, but insects can be bothersome, so here is a modern version of 'Vinegar of the Four Thieves'.

2 tablespoons of *Rosmarinus officinalis* (rosemary)
2 tablespoons of *Salvia officinalis* (sage)
2 tablespoons of *Lavandula angustifolia* (lavender)
2 tablespoons of *Ruta graveoloens* (rue)
2 tablespoons of *Mentha* x *piperata* (peppermint)
Enough apple cider vinegar to cover the herbs completely

To make the herb vinegar, simply chop the herbs and put them in lidded jar. Pour the vinegar over the herbs, put the lid on, and leave to infuse for three or four days. Strain the vinegar into a plastic spray bottle and use on the skin or on surfaces, as required.

CLOTHES MOTHS

My grandma's best coat reeked of moth balls. Or rather it reeked of what moth balls were made from, namely naphthalene. I use the past tense on purpose because the use of naphthalene-based mothballs is now banned in the UK and elsewhere; bearing in mind naphthalene is both toxic and flammable, this is hardly surprising. But what can you use instead of those pungent discs to rid your home of that voracious pest, the clothes moth *Tineola bisselliella*?

Arguably you can do nothing. It is near impossible to be purged of them entirely. Our modern homes, which are warm all year round and contain lots of natural fibres for them to feed on, provide an ideal breeding ground. That, and the fact that we rarely give our homes a deep, spring clean any more, means that the moths are free to reproduce virtually *ad infinitum*.

Other than getting professional pest controllers in and keeping all our clothes in pest-proof bags when we are not wearing them, the best we can hope to do is deter the female moth from laying her eggs in our prize cashmere sweaters. Fortunately there are a number of herbs that keep moths at bay. Among them are *Chamaemelum nobile* (Roman chamomile) or *Matricaria recutita* (German chamomile), *Tanacetum parthenium* (feverfew), *Lavandula angustifolia* (lavender), *Mentha* x *piperata* (peppermint), *Rosmarinus officinalis* (rosemary), *Galium odoratum* (sweet woodruff), *Tanacetum vulgare* (tansy) and *Artemisia abrotanum* (southernwood).

Choose a number of different dried herbs and add a couple of cloves (the spice, not garlic!), pop them in a bag made from loose- or fine-weave fabric, such as muslin, so that the aroma can circulate – approximately 10cm square is ideal – and position the bags in drawers and wardrobes. You could also create pretty sachets from embroidered organza or muslin. Either way, the more bags or sachets you use, the stronger the fragrance and the better the protection.

ANTS

Just as herbs won't eradicate flies and moths, there is no herb that will kill off ants. Like flies and moths, however, there are certain herbs whose scent ants are not partial to, including *Mentha pulegium* (pennyroyal), *Ruta graveoloens* (rue) and *Tanacetum vulgare* (tansy). I don't mind ants in the garden, within reason, but I do object to them invading the house. If you have ants in the house and you know where they have gained access, try spreading some slightly crushed herbs at the entrance to deter them from coming any further.

MICE

Mice, too, dislike the scent of some herbs. Hopefully you will never have to deal with them inside your home, but like many people I have had them in the garage and shed. I know they have to live somewhere but bearing in mind that mice are incontinent I am not at all happy to give them board and lodging. I have found that numerous bunches of *Mentha spicata* (spearmint) and *Tanacetum vulgare* (tansy), placed strategically at possible access holes and creating a barrier around my stored apples and the like, does keep them at bay.

If, on the other hand, mice prove to be a real problem and cannot be deterred there is a herb that can help. It does rely on the premise that you want to lure the mice into a trap and dispose of the creatures as you see fit. Apparently they can't resist *Pimpinella anisum* (aniseed). So bait your trap with aniseed – and wait.

# Preserving Wraps

If you grow your own apples and pears and wish to store them to use later, a good way to help prolong their 'shelf life' is to wrap them individually in dried nettle leaves. Gather big leaves – make sure you wear sting-proof gloves of course – and lay them out on a frame to dry (see page 30). Then carefully wrap each fruit in leaves and put them in a storage crate, making sure that they are not touching one another. They will keep for two to three months or longer depending on the type and variety of fruit.

# Dyeing

Is there no end to the versatility of herbs! You can even extract colour from them. Indeed you can obtain colour from almost any plant – but some will result in more pleasing shades and hues than others. In fact until the relatively recent introduction of chemical-based dyes, plants provided the only source of dye.

Some people still prefer the 'natural' colour that can be obtained from plant-based dyes, so if you do too, it is worth growing some of your own dye plants. The obvious herbs to grow for dyeing are those whose Latin species name includes *tinctoria* or *tinctorium*, which means that that they can be used for dyeing or staining (from the Latin *tingere* – to colour), such as *Anthemis tinctoria* (dyer's chamomile) or *Carthamus tinctorius* (safflower).

In addition you can use other common herbs, such as *Tanacetum vulgare* (tansy) and *Achillea millefolium* (yarrow). If dyeing your own material or yarn is something you fancy doing it is well worth experimenting with a whole range of herbs to see which colours you like. I have had a go at dyeing a piece of cotton with *Carthamus tinctorius* (safflower) and I cannot begin to tell you what a thrill it was to see my material turn a beautiful shade of yellow before my very eyes. If only chemistry lessons at school had been this exciting I might have made a half-decent scientist!

After you have harvested your plant material you can either use it fresh, or dry it to use later (see page 30). There are no hard-and-fast rules about the amount of dyestuff you will need, but a general rule of thumb is you should use the same weight of dyestuff as the weight of fibre you are dyeing. So, for example, if you want to dye 100g of fibre, then you will need 100g of dyestuff in the form of petals, leaves, or whatever part of your plant is used. Some dyes also need a mordant (see page 112).

EXTRACTING THE COLOUR

To extract the colour from the plant material you will need to immerse it in water and then heat it very gently for about an hour. Again, there are no exact times: much depends on the plant material itself but I allowed the *Carthamus tinctorius* (safflower) to heat for just over an hour, about 70 minutes. Turn off the heat and allow the liquid to cool before you strain it. It is now ready to be used.

MORDANTING

Some dyes need a mordant – an extra ingredient – to act as a link between the material and the dyestuff so that the dye becomes permanently 'fixed' to the material being dyed. The final colour of your dye can vary depending on what mordant you use. For example, an aluminium mordant will give you bright, clear colours, whereas an iron mordant will give a darker tone.

There are two categories of mordant: chemical and natural. The most common chemical mordants are aluminium, copper and ferrous (iron); they can all be bought in powder or crystal form (including instructions!) from a dyestuff supplier. These are suitable for all fibres, both animal (such as wool) and plant (such as linen).

The most frequently used plant mordants are tannin, high concentrations of which can be found in the leaves of *Rhus typhina* (stag's horn sumac), and oxalic acid which can be found in *Rheum rhabarbarum* (rhubarb) leaves. Please remember that oxalic acid is a poison and care should be taken with its use – on no account ingest it. Tannin is more suitable for plant fibres, and oxalic acid for animal fibres. To extract the tannin or acid, simply put the plant material in a pan and cover it with water. Then simmer it for about an hour and strain off the liquid: this is your mordant solution.

The most effective way to mordant your fabric or fibre is to carry out the process before you dye it. This means submerging your fabric in a mordant solution, usually with heat, and then letting it cool, still submerged, overnight. You must then take the fabric out of the mordant 'bath' and rinse it thoroughly in cold water. The fabric can then be dried and stored until you wish to dye it. Don't forget to make a note of which mordant you used.

METHODS OF DYEING

*Cool*

Cool dyeing is the most straightforward method, although it may not always be the most successful. (Some dyestuff needs heat to be properly 'activated'.) You simply take your fibre or fabric (mordanted if necessary) and soak it in water for up to two hours to make sure that all the material is thoroughly wetted. Then put the wet material into a pot containing the dyeing liquid (the dye bath), making sure that the material is completely submerged and that it has enough room to move around freely. You should leave the bath overnight and check the next day to see how much dye the material has taken up. If the colour is not as strong as you would like, leave it for longer – several days if required. Remove the fabric from the dye bath, let it dry and then rinse in clean, cold water.

*Hot*

As with the cool dyeing method, your fibre or fabric has to be completely wet before you put it into the dye bath. For hot dyeing you will, of course, have to use a metal pot, preferably made from stainless steel. Gradually bring the dye bath to simmering point, moving the fabric around gently from time to time, and heat for at least 30 minutes, and possibly up to an hour, depending on the depth of colour you require. Turn off the heat and allow the bath to cool to room temperature before you don your rubber gloves and remove the fabric.

Allow the material to dry and then rinse in clean, cold water to remove excess dye.

# Gazetteer of Herbs
## Mentioned in the Book

Information about hardiness categories can be found in Appendix 1 on page 179.

### Achillea millefolium

Common names: Yarrow, staunchweed, soldier's woundwort, bloodwort

| | |
|---|---|
| Type of plant/hardiness | Herbaceous perennial/H4 – hardy |
| Height and spread | Up to 90cm/40–60cm |
| Best position | Full sun |
| Soil | Fertile, well drained |
| Method(s) of propagation | By cuttings in early summer; by division in early autumn |
| Part of plant used | Whole plant |
| Harvest | Gather the whole plant in summer to dry |
| USES | |
| *Medicinally* | Externally: for wounds and nosebleeds |
| *Cosmetically* | As a skin cleanser |
| *In the home* | As a dye |

There are a multitude of vernacular names for *Achillea*, the most common being yarrow. But it is also known as soldier's woundwort, staunchweed and bloodwort, names which point to its use as a medicinal herb to heal wounds and staunch the flow of blood. According to myth, the plant takes its name from Achilles, who ordered it to be used to heal the injuries of his soldiers after the siege of Troy, and whose only vulnerable spot in an otherwise invincible body, was, well, his Achilles' heel!

Many myths are also associated with *Achillea*: you can tie it to your baby's cradle to prevent its soul being stolen; carry a sachet of *Achillea* about your person and you will attract lasting friendship; sleep with a sprig under your pillow and you will dream of your true love. I'm not sure whether any or all of these would actually work, but stranger things have happened, I'm sure!

Although the flower of the 'wild' *Achillea* is a rather nondescript chalky white colour the cultivated hybrids have some subtle and striking hues which lend themselves to most garden settings. Most varieties will fade in colour, however, as the blooms mature.

### *Allium sativum*

Common name: Garlic

| | |
|---|---|
| Type of plant/hardiness | Bulb/H4 – hardy |
| Height and spread | 45cm/25cm |
| Best position | Full sun |
| Soil | Fertile, well drained |
| Method(s) of propagation | Plant individual cloves in autumn/winter |
| Part of plant used | Bulbs |
| Harvest | Lift bulbs in summer to early autumn |
| USES | |
| *Medicinally* | Externally: for skin problems and bacterial infection |
| | Internally: to treat colds; reputed to reduce blood pressure and cholesterol levels |

Everyone knows garlic, if only for its pungent aroma! Its most common usage is probably in cooking, since it adds a another layer of flavour to a multitude of dishes. It has also been used for millennia as a home remedy due to its antimicrobial properties. From the Egyptians, who used it to prevent colds and bronchial conditions, to the Russians in the

Second World War for whom it was an important antiseptic, garlic has earned its place as an invaluable addition to our medicinal herb garden.

### *Aloe vera* (synonym *Aloe barbadensis*)

| | |
|---|---|
| Type of plant/hardiness | Evergreen perennial/H1b – subtropical |
| Height and spread | 60cm/30cm although growth is restricted if grown in a pot |
| Best position | Full sun |
| Soil | Well drained |
| Method(s) of propagation | By offsets at any time |
| Part of plant used | Sap from the stem |
| Harvest | As required |
| USES | |
| *Medicinally* | Externally: for burns; scalds; sunburn; eczema; acne |
| *Cosmetically* | In hand and body creams |

As a medicinal herb, *Aloe vera* has a long pedigree. It is mentioned in the Egyptian Ebers Papyrus dating from 1552 BCE and it reappears periodically throughout recorded history. It appears to have been introduced to Europe during the tenth century. It is a native of South Africa, Arabia and the Cape Verde Islands; this gives us an idea about the sort of growing conditions it needs. A minimum temperature of 10°C is required, along with full sun and free draining soil.

The only successful way to grow it in Britain is on a windowsill indoors or in a heated greenhouse. I keep mine on the kitchen windowsill where it is handy in case of burns: the sap from a snapped-off leaf will give instant relief to an oven burn or minor scald. It is the polysaccharides in the sap which are thought to reduce inflammation of the skin and aid healing.

***Aloysia triphylla*** (synonym *Aloysia citriodora*)
Common name: Lemon verbena

| | |
|---|---|
| Type of plant/hardiness | Deciduous sub-shrub/H3 – half hardy |
| Height and spread | 2.5m/2.5m |
| Best position | Sun |
| Soil | Light, well drained |
| Method(s) of propagation | By softwood cuttings in summer |
| Part of plant used | Leaves |
| Harvest | Pick leaves in summer to use fresh, or dry |
| USES | |
| *Medicinally* | Externally: for acne and boils |
| | Internally: as a refreshing drink |
| *In the home* | In pot pourri |
| ☠ BEWARE ☠ | Can increase sensitivity to sun |

Whenever I close my eyes and crush a leaf of lemon verbena, it takes me straight back to the Saturday mornings of my childhood when my sister and I would be given a pack of sweets each of which always contained a lemon sherbet – complete with liquorice dipper. The tantalising citrus tang will stay with me forever: it is one of my 'scents of memory': Proust has his *petites madeleines*, I have, amongst others, my lemon sherbet/verbena.

Nowadays I tend to use lemon verbena in my herb pot pourri, but occasionally I have a cup of lemon verbena tea, which is very relaxing.

Lemon verbena was first introduced to England in 1784: being a native of South America it came via Spain, the colonial power of the day, as part of what has become known as the 'South American Exchange' trading network. It is a half hardy, verging on tender, plant, needing protection in the winter. For this reason I grow mine in a pot which can be moved under cover over the dormant season. I also cover it with some horticultural fleece to be on the safe side.

### *Althaea officinalis*
Common name: Marshmallow

| | |
|---|---|
| Type of plant/hardiness | Herbaceous perennial/H4 – hardy |
| Height and spread | 2m/90cm |
| Best position | Sun |
| Soil | Prefers moist soil |
| Method(s) of propagation | Gather ripe seed in late summer and sow immediately (germination can be erratic); by division in autumn |
| Part of plant used | Leaves, roots |
| Harvest | Pick leaves in summer to use fresh, or dry. Harvest roots from established plants to dry |
| USES | |
| *Medicinally* | Externally: for acne and boils<br>Internally: for coughs and catarrh |

Whenever I come across *Althaea* it reminds me of an old lady who lived in our village. She always carried a bag of marshmallows in her pocket and gave us children one whenever we saw her. She told us that she picked them from her marshmallow bush, pointing towards the pale pink-flowered plant next to her front door. Apparently, the fairies would come at dead of night and sprinkle their magic dust over the flowers, turning them instantly into marshmallows which she then picked before anyone else was up. I found out much later that marshmallows are actually made from the root and not the flowers of *Althaea officinalis* – besides which her marshmallows looked remarkably similar to the ones Mr Joe sold at the village shop!

It's true that the root can indeed be made into marshmallow sweeties, but it, and the leaves, can also be used for bronchial complaints and to alleviate coughs and catarrh.

And, as if that wasn't enough, the flowers are very attractive to bees and other pollinating insects – which in my book is even more reason to grow it!

### *Anethum graveolens*
Common name: Dill

| | |
|---|---|
| Type of plant/hardiness | Annual/H4 – hardy |
| Height and spread | 90cm/30cm |
| Best position | Sun |
| Soil | Well drained but moisture retentive |
| Method(s) of propagation | By seed outdoors in spring |
| Part of plant used | Leaves, seeds |
| Harvest | Cut leaves in spring and summer |
| | Gather seeds in summer |
| USES | |
| *Medicinally* | Internally: for digestive disorders |
| *Cosmetically* | Dill oil can be used in soaps and detergents |

Dill originated in southern Europe, the Middle East or western Asia, depending on which book you read! Suffice it to say that dill can now be found throughout the world and has naturalised in many areas. It was certainly used, and highly regarded, by the ancient Greeks and Romans and it is mentioned in St Matthew's gospel as being used to pay tithes. Later, in the seventeenth century, Culpepper writes that dill 'is used in medicines that serve to expel wind, and the pains proceeding therefrom'.

Dill is easily grown from seed, and does not like being transplanted, so sow it where you want it to grow. Although it is hardy it appreciates a sunny position with some shelter from the wind. Its feathery leaves resemble fennel but its flavour is quite different: dill has a mild, warm flavour, whilst fennel has more of an aniseed taste.

### *Anthemis tinctoria*

Common name: Dyer's chamomile

| | |
|---|---|
| Type of plant/hardiness | Herbaceous perennial/H4 – hardy |
| Height and spread | 60cm/60cm |
| Best position | Sun |
| Soil | Will tolerate most well drained soils |
| Method(s) of propagation | By seed in spring; by division in spring; by basal root cuttings in late spring or summer |
| Part of plant used | Flowers |
| Harvest | Pick flower heads as they open to dry |
| USES | |
| *In the home* | As a dye |

*Anthemis tinctoria* is a hardy perennial plant which is historically extremely important as a dye plant, especially in Turkey where threads were dyed to use in carpets. The daisy-like flower heads produce dyes of various shades of yellow and green. It self-seeds freely and tolerates most soils except where it is waterlogged. Apart from the original species, which has bright yellow flowers, new varieties have been developed especially for the herbaceous border: these include *A. tinctoria* 'E.C. Buxton' and *A. tinctoria* 'Sauce Hollandaise' with lemon-yellow and cream flowers respectively. They all have the same active constituents, though.

### *Arnica montana*
Common name: Arnica

| | |
|---|---|
| Type of plant/hardiness | Rhizomatous perennial/H4 – hardy |
| Height and spread | Up to 60cm/15cm |
| Best position | Sun |
| Soil | Well drained, humus rich, acid |
| Method(s) of propagation | By seed in autumn; by division in spring |
| Part of plant used | Flowers |
| Harvest | Pick flower heads when fully open to dry |
| USES | |
| *Medicinally* | Externally: for bruises; sprains; and chilblains |
| ☠ BEWARE ☠ | See below |

Probably the first thing to say is that although Arnica is widely available as a commercially produced topical cream which is completely safe to use, the plant also has highly toxic properties and should not be taken internally. Having said that, it is widely used in Germany for heart conditions but in the UK it can only be used externally, and in the USA its use is prohibited entirely. So, having given you lots of information about its ideal growing conditions, when you should harvest it, and so on, I am now urging you to forget all that and buy your Arnica cream from the chemist!

### *Artemisia abrotanum*

Common names: Southernwood, lad's love

| | |
|---|---|
| Type of plant/hardiness | Semi-evergreen sub-shrub/H4 – hardy |
| Height and spread | Up to 1m/60cm |
| Best position | Sun or light shade |
| Soil | Well drained |
| Method(s) of propagation | By seed in spring; by semi hardwood cuttings in late summer |
| Part of plant used | Leaves |
| Harvest | Pick leaves before flowering to dry |
| USES | |
| *Medicinally* | Externally: for frostbite and swelling; to extract splinters |
| *In the home* | As an insect repellent |

This *Artemisia* has been used for centuries as an insect repellent. It was one of the must-have plants in the tussie mussies, or nosegays (see page 102), that people would carry to keep nasty smells and insects at bay. And during the time of the plague doctors would attempt to protect themselves from contagion by wearing beak-like masks filled with herbs of all kinds, and *Artemisia abrotanum* would certainly have been among their number.

It is also reputed to have cured baldness, or at least prevented complete loss of hair. According to Culpepper: 'the ashes mingled with old salad oil helps those that have their hair fallen and are bald, causing the hair to grow again.' I have tried to persuade a friend of mine who is a little hirsutely challenged to daub his pate with such a preparation to test its efficacy, but he remains emphatically against the idea! Oh well.

### *Borago officinalis*

Common names: Borage, starflower

| | |
|---|---|
| Type of plant/hardiness | Annual/H4 – hardy |
| Height and spread | 50cm/50cm |
| Best position | Sun or part shade |
| Soil | Well drained |
| Method(s) of propagation | By seed in spring, or leave to self-seed |
| Part of plant used | Leaves and flowers |
| Harvest | Pick leaves and flowers as required – they do not dry well |
| USES | |
| *Medicinally* | Externally: for skin conditions Internally: to bring down fevers; to alleviate mouth and throat infections Also available in a commercially produced preparation as an alternative to evening primrose oil |

*Borage officinalis* oil, when known by its common name of starflower oil, is becoming better known as an alternative to evening primrose (*Oenothera biennis*) oil, both of which contain gamma linolenic acid (GLA), an omega-6 unsaturated fatty acid, vital for general health.

Borage leaves and flowers (separated from the calyx, which is rather bitter) are also tasty, and colourful, ingredients in Pimms, the refreshing summer drink.

### *Calendula officinalis*
Common name: Pot marigold

| | |
|---|---|
| Type of plant/hardiness | Annual/H4 – hardy |
| Height and spread | 50cm/50cm |
| Best position | Sun or part shade |
| Soil | Well drained |
| Method(s) of propagation | By seed in spring, or leave to self-seed |
| Part of plant used | Whole flowers and petals |
| Harvest | Pick flowers as required to use fresh or dry |
| USES | |
| *Medicinally* | Externally: for skin conditions; to aid healing |
| *Cosmetically* | In hand and body creams and lotions, and in soap |
| *In the home* | In pot pourri; as a dye |

Whenever I look at *Calendula*, I have to smile. It's one of those cheery, bright and breezy flowers that do you good just by being there. Indeed, as a healing herb it is almost unsurpassed: it's good for minor burns, injuries and wounds, and for a multitude of skin conditions from dry skin to nappy rash, and fungal infections too, such as athlete's foot. Containing a variety of antibacterial, antifungal, antibiotic and antiseptic properties, it really should be a staple in every herb garden.

### Carthamus tinctorius

Common names: Safflower, saffron thistle, false saffron

| | |
|---|---|
| Type of plant/hardiness | Annual/H4 – hardy |
| Height and spread | 60cm/30cm |
| Best position | Sun |
| Soil | Well drained |
| Method(s) of propagation | By seed in spring when temperature is 10–15°C |
| Part of plant used | Flowers |
| Harvest | Pick flowers as required to use fresh or dry |
| USES | |
| *Medicinally* | Externally: for bruising; sprains; wounds; skin inflammations |
| | Internally: for coronary artery disease – consult a qualified practitioner |
| *In the home* | As a dye; food colouring |

Both the genus name of *Carthamus* and the species name *tinctorius* give us a clue as to the main use of this herb: *Carthamus* comes from the Arabic *qurtom* or the Hebrew *qarthami*, both of which mean 'to paint'; *tinctorius* comes from the Latin *tingere*, to colour, so it's undeniable that this herb was, and still is, used as a colouring agent or dye. Indeed it is traditionally used to dye the robes of Buddhist monks and nuns. It is completely safe to use in edible products and as such is used as a colouring in dairy produce, confectionary and liqueurs.

*Carthamus* is also a useful herb to include in any cream to help skin conditions.

### Chamaemelum nobile

Common name: Roman chamomile

| | |
|---|---|
| Type of plant/hardiness | Perennial/H4 – hardy |
| Height and spread | Up to 50cm/50cm |
| Best position | Sun |
| Soil | Light, well drained |
| Method(s) of propagation | By seed in spring or autumn; by division in spring |
| Part of plant used | Flowers |
| Harvest | Pick flowers as required to use fresh or dry |
| USES | |
| *Medicinally* | Externally: for sore skin |
| | Internally: to aid relaxation; for digestive disorders |
| *Cosmetically* | In shampoo to lighten the hair |

The herb chamomile is almost certainly best known as a tea, and I think it's probable that many of us first came across it when that scamp Peter Rabbit was sent to bed with a dose of it after attracting the wrath of Mr McGregor. It's not clear in Beatrix Potter's story if this was as a punishment or whether Mrs Rabbit knew her stuff about calming herbs! I would like to think it is the latter because Peter was asleep in no time at all. Either way, it certainly encourages relaxation and is good for the digestion.

Chamomile is also a useful addition to shampoo, especially if you have blonde hair.

### *Daucus carota*

Common name: Wild carrot

| | |
|---|---|
| Type of plant/hardiness | Biennial/H4 – hardy |
| Height and spread | 30cm/25cm |
| Best position | Sun or partial shade |
| Soil | Light, well drained |
| Method(s) of propagation | By seed in spring, summer or autumn |
| Part of plant used | Roots and seeds |
| Harvest | Dig roots as required; harvest seeds when ripe |

USES

| | |
|---|---|
| *Medicinally* | Internally: juiced roots soothe the digestive tract |
| *Cosmetically* | Crushed seeds can be used in skin creams |
| *In the home* | As a dye |

I wonder how many of us were told as youngsters that if we diligently eat our carrots, we will see much better in the dark? Some people dismiss this as an old wife's (or should it be old mum's) tale, and although it's not strictly accurate, there is a grain of truth in it because carrots do contain beta-carotene, which the body can convert into Vitamin A, one of the vitamins needed for healthy vision.

Carrots are members of the Apiaceae family, all of which have quite similar feathery leaves and flat-topped or mounded inflorescences made up of many individual flowers: the characteristic that sets the wild carrot apart is the tiny maroon-red flower right in the centre of the inflorescence.

### *Echinacea* species
Common name: Coneflower

| | |
|---|---|
| Type of plant/hardiness | Perennial/H4 – hardy |
| Height and spread | 60cm/40cm |
| Best position | Sun |
| Soil | Deep, humus rich, well drained |
| Method(s) of propagation | By seed in spring; by root cuttings in the dormant season |
| Part of plant used | Roots |
| Harvest | Dig roots in the autumn to dry |
| USES | |
| *Medicinally* | Externally: for skin disorders and wounds |
| | Internally: for early stages of coughs and colds; skin diseases and fungal infections; as a gargle for sore throats |

*Echinacea* comes from the Greek, *echinos*, which roughly translated means 'spiny'. The centre of *Echinacea* does indeed feel slightly prickly or spiny and this is the key way of telling it apart from *Rudbeckia* (which shares the common name of coneflower), the centre of which is much softer.

Three species of *Echinacea* – *E. purpurea*, *E. angustifolia*, and *E. pallida* – have long been used as medicinal herbs, particularly in North America. The active ingredients are many and complicated; suffice it to say that they are known to stimulate the immune system, promote healing and have anti-viral and anti- bacterial properties. Besides all that, *Echinacea* is worth growing in the garden simply because it has an attractive flower and is beloved by bees and other pollinating insects.

## *Equisetum arvense*
Common name: Horsetail

| | |
|---|---|
| Type of plant/hardiness | Perennial/H4 – hardy |
| Height and spread | 20-80cm/indefinite |
| Best position | Sun or partial shade |
| Soil | Moist, but will grow just about anywhere |
| Method(s) of propagation | By division in early spring |
| Part of plant used | Stems |
| Harvest | Cut stems as required during growing season to dry |
| USES | |
| *Cosmetically* | In shampoos and conditioners |
| *In the home* | Effective as a pan scourer |

Having given you lots of information about growing horsetail, why anyone would want to actually cultivate it is beyond me! It is highly invasive and difficult to get rid of: this isn't surprising, since the root system can penetrate down to thirty feet and it has survived as a genus since the Carboniferous era – approximately 360 to 300 million years ago. So what I'm really saying is, don't bother to grow it yourself because you will find plentiful supplies in hedgerows, growing through pavements, and in other people's gardens, if you don't already have it in your own, that is!

Another, less common, name for *Equisetum* is Pewterwort. Gerard, in his *Herbal* of 1597, tells us that it was used for cleaning pewter and other kitchen utensils – so my suggestion for using it as a pan scourer (see page 96) has a distinguished pedigree!

### *Foeniculum vulgare*
Common name: Fennel

| | |
|---|---|
| Type of plant/hardiness | Perennial/H4 – hardy |
| Height and spread | Up to 1m/45cm |
| Best position | Sun |
| Soil | Fertile, moist but well drained |
| Method(s) of propagation | By seed outdoors in spring |
| Part of plant used | Leaves, seeds and roots |
| Harvest | Gather leaves as required; collect seeds in autumn; lift roots in autumn to dry |
| USES | |
| *Medicinally* | Externally: as a mouthwash |
| | Internally: for indigestion and wind |
| | Traditionally, seeds were chewed during Lent to allay hunger |
| *In the home* | In air fresheners |

It's amazing the sort of snippets of information you pick up along life's road. No, I'm not going all philosophical on you, and I'm not going to give you a list of things that, once I've told you, you'll wish I hadn't! The only piece of, arguably useless, information I would like to share with you now is to do with fennel.

When my long-suffering husband and I visited Madeira for the first time a few years ago we went on the obligatory 'round the island' trip, starting and finishing in Funchal, the capital. The first thing I learned about that fascinating island is that Funchal was so named because of the abundance of wild fennel growing in the vicinity. Apparently the Portuguese for fennel is *funcho*; take the *o* away and add *al* and we have 'a plantation of fennel'.

Now you may wonder what this has to do with growing fennel here in the UK. The point I want to make is that, as with just about every other type of plant, if you can replicate the conditions, in both soil and climate, which it has in its 'wild' surroundings, then the chances are that your attempt at growing it will be successful. So, if you can provide your fennel with Madeira-type conditions during our growing season then your crop will not only survive; it will, hopefully, thrive, possibly even to the extent that it becomes a nuisance. In fact, in parts of Australia, it has become so prolific that it is subject to statutory control as a weed.

Do not grow it near dill as they will hybridise and their offspring are of no value either as herbs or ornamentals.

Folklore has it that if you hang a bunch of fennel above your door on Midsummer's Eve then you will be protected from enchantment and witches – very handy if you are plagued by 'trick or treaters' at Hallowe'en!

### *Fragaria vesca*

Common names: Wild strawberry, Alpine strawberry

| | |
|---|---|
| Type of plant/hardiness | Perennial (see below)/H4 – hardy |
| Height and spread | 20cm/indefinite |
| Best position | Sun or part shade |
| Soil | Rich, neutral to alkaline |
| Method(s) of propagation | By seed in spring; by stolons in spring |
| Part of plant used | Leaves, fruit and roots |
| Harvest | Gather leaves in summer and dry; pick fruit as required; lift roots in autumn to dry |

USES

| | |
|---|---|
| *Medicinally* | Externally: for sunburn |
| | Internally: for diarrhoea; stomach upsets; and gout |
| *Cosmetically* | For skin blemishes; as a teeth whitener |

*Fragaria vesca* is not the large, cultivated strawberry that, served with cream, reminds us that Wimbledon is underway and summer is at last with us. It is, rather, the much smaller, wild strawberry which was first mentioned in England in a tenth-century plant list. The fruit of wild strawberry is more fragrant and flavourful than the cultivated strawberry – pop one in your mouth and you get an explosion of delicate aroma and fruity sapidity.

A tisane made from the leaves and roots will ease the symptoms of diarrhoea and other stomach upsets, and a cloth soaked in the same tisane will help sunburn.

Because the fruit contains malic acid it helps prevent discolouration of the teeth.

Although *Fragaria* are perennial plants, they will deteriorate after three years or so. Nurture some offspring which are produced from the parent plant to act as replacements.

### *Galium odoratum*
Common name: Sweet woodruff

| | |
|---|---|
| Type of plant/hardiness | Perennial/H4 – hardy |
| Height and spread | 50cm/indefinite |
| Best position | Partial shade |
| Soil | Moist, but well drained |

| | |
|---|---|
| Method(s) of propagation | By seed; by division of rhizomes in early spring or autumn |
| Part of plant used | Leaves and flowers |
| Harvest | Cut the plants when in flower to dry |
| USES | |
| *In the home* | In pot pourri |

There are conflicting reports as to whether this *Galium* is safe to use for medicinal purposes, so I have deliberately chosen to recommend it for use in the home only.

The species name *odoratum* of this *Galium* gives us a clue to its main attribute – it smells nice! If, when you gather it, you find little discernible scent, don't worry – its potency intensifies when it is dried. In this form it finds its way into pot pourri and was used for centuries as a strewing herb to keep bugs at bay and to release its fragrance when trodden on.

It is also useful as a dye plant, giving a red dye from the root, and soft tan to grey-green dyes from the stems and leaves.

### *Glycyrrhiza glabra*
Common names: Liquorice, sweet root

| | |
|---|---|
| Type of plant/hardiness | Perennial/H4 – hardy |
| Height and spread | 1m/1m |
| Best position | Partial shade |
| Soil | Deep, rich, moisture retentive but not water logged |
| Method(s) of propagation | By division in autumn or spring; by stolons in spring |
| Part of plant used | Roots and stolons |
| Harvest | Lift roots and stolons in early autumn to dry. Do not harvest before the plant |

is established, usually three years after planting

USES

*Medicinally*      Because of the many and varied contraindications care should be taken

Like many herbs, liquorice has a long pedigree and we know that it was imported to England in the thirteenth century. By the mid-1500s it was also being grown here, mainly to be made into a medicine to help alleviate stomach and intestinal problems, but also as a sweetener – hence its common name of sweet root. In fact liquorice is best known as a confection – who hasn't heard of Bassett's Liquorice Allsorts? These evolved from the famous Pontefract cakes, a solid disc of liquorice, produced in and around the Yorkshire town of Pontefract from 1760. At one time there were more than a dozen liquorice factories; now there are but two left.

Despite giving you information about how to grow and harvest liquorice, you should be very careful when it comes to using it, especially for medicinal purposes. If, like me, you like liquorice, be content to buy it from the sweetie shop!

### *Hamamelis virginiana*
Common name: Witch hazel

| | |
|---|---|
| Type of plant/Hardiness | Deciduous shrub/H4 – hardy |
| Height and spread | 5m/4m |
| Best position | Sun or part shade |
| Soil | Moist, humus rich, neutral to slightly acid |

| Method(s) of propagation | Can be grown by seed but best method is by stolons |
|---|---|
| Part of plant used | Leaves, twigs |
| Harvest | Pick leaves in summer; cut twigs in spring |

USES

| *Medicinally* | Externally: for skin conditions Internally: for diarrhoea and haemorrhoids |
|---|---|
| *Cosmetically* | In skin creams and facial cleansers and toners |
| ☙ BEWARE ☙ | Avoid long-term use: the high tannin content may be carcinogenic; prolonged topical use may cause dermatitis |

Despite its common name, *Hamamelis* is not a hazel. It gained this name when American colonists started using it to divine water, just as they had back home with hazel twigs. And apparently the name witch is a distortion of the Anglo-Saxon word '*wyche*' meaning bend. So there we have it!

*Hamamelis* bark has a very high tannin content which is apparently responsible for its astringent qualities. These qualities are highly prized in some lotions and tonics, but the plant should be used with care (see above). Rather than creating your own infusion you may like to buy distilled witch hazel water, which is widely available and has all of the benefits with none of the risks.

**Hypericum perforatum**

Common name: St John's wort

| | |
|---|---|
| Type of plant/Hardiness | Semi-evergreen perennial/H4 – hardy |
| Height and spread | 30–90cm/30cm |
| Best position | Sun |
| Soil | Moist, well drained. Prefers slightly alkaline conditions |
| Method(s) of propagation | By seed sown in spring or autumn; by division in early autumn |
| Part of plant used | Stem, leaves, flowers |
| Harvest | Cut stems as flowering begins |
| USES | |
| *Medicinally* | Externally: for burns; bruises; cramps; sprains; tennis elbow; wounds |
| | Internally: for anxiety; menopausal symptoms; shingles |
| *Cosmetically* | In hand and body creams |
| *In the home* | As a dye |
| ☠ BEWARE ☠ | Harmful if eaten. Can increase sensitivity to sun. Should not be taken by people who are chronically depressed |

There are more than 400 *Hypericum* species, but the one we are interested in is *H. perforatum*, the common St John's wort, so called, some say, because it flowers around St John's Day (Midsummer's day, 24th June).

St John's wort has long been used to treat nervous complaints and as a potent healing herb: for example, 'red oil' (see page 56), made with olive oil and *H. perforatum* flowers, is an effective treatment for burns and wounds. More recently, clinical trials have shown that its active ingredients *hypericin* and *hyperforin* are efficacious in relieving mild depression, to the extent that it has been described as 'nature's Prozac', although it is not prescribed for severe or chronic depression.

The plant itself is attractive with yellow, open flowers and prominent stamens. The leaves, when held up to the light, show translucent dots on the underside – this 'pinprick' characteristic is what gives it the name *perforatum*.

### *Hyssopus officinalis*
Common name: Hyssop

| | |
|---|---|
| Type of plant/Hardiness | Semi-evergreen perennial/H4 – hardy |
| Height and spread | 60cm/60cm |
| Best position | Sun |
| Soil | Well drained, verging on dry. Can tolerate slightly alkaline conditions |
| Method(s) of propagation | By seed in autumn; by softwood cuttings in summer |
| Part of plant used | Leaves, flowers |
| Harvest | Pick leaves as required; pick flowers as the buds start to open |
| USES | |
| *Medicinally* | Internally: for respiratory problems |
| *In the home* | In pot pourri |
| ☠ BEWARE ☠ | Hyssop essential oil is subject to legal restrictions in some countries and should not be used internally unless prescribed by a professional |

Hyssop is native to southern Europe, the Near East and southern Russia. Its reputation goes back to antiquity when it was used as a medicinal or purifying herb. Hyssop could always be found in monastery gardens where it was grown as a 'cure-all' for diverse complaints from acne to worms. Indeed, Gerard, in his herbal of 1597, left hyssop 'altogether without description, as being a plant so well knowne that it needeth none'. Nowadays its application is far less all-encompassing and it is used more-or-less as an ingredient to ease respiratory problems and bronchitis.

Hyssop is a sun worshipper and must have well-drained soil. It makes an ideal low hedge: trim back the flowers, which can be blue, pink or white, depending on the variety, in the autumn, and in spring give the plants a 'haircut' to keep them in shape. It also makes a perfect container plant.

### *Iris germanica* var. *florentina*
Common name: Orris

| | |
|---|---|
| Type of plant/Hardiness | Rhizomatous perennial/H4 – hardy |
| Height and spread | Up to 1m/indefinite |
| Best position | Sun |
| Soil | Well drained, neutral to alkaline |
| Method(s) of propagation | By division of rhizomes after flowering |
| Part of plant used | Rhizomes |
| Harvest | Lift rhizomes in late summer or early autumn to dry |

**USES**

| | |
|---|---|
| *Medicinally* | Internally: for coughs and colds |
| *In the home* | As a fixative in pot pourri |
| ☙ BEWARE ☙ | All parts of *Iris* species are potentially toxic if eaten. Can cause skin irritation |

There has been doubt over the correct name for this Iris for years. Some maintain that it is a separate species entirely and should be called *Iris florentina*, while others say it is a cultivar of *Iris germanica*. Either way, this is the Iris from which orris powder is obtained. Orris powder is, and always has been, an important ingredient in pot pourri and perfumes, 'fixing' the scent and making the fragrance last longer.

The rhizome has also been used as an expectorant to alleviate coughs and colds, although there are other, more efficacious, remedies.

### *Isatis tinctoria*
Common name: Woad

| | |
|---|---|
| Type of plant/Hardiness | Biennial or short-lived perennial/H4 – hardy |
| Height and spread | 60cm/45cm |
| Best position | Sun |
| Soil | Rich, well drained. Prefers slightly alkaline conditions |
| Method(s) of propagation | By seed sown in autumn or spring – as it is a member of the Brassicaceae family, you should not grow it for more than two years in the same soil |
| Part of plant used | Leaves, roots |
| Harvest | Pick leaves in summer to use fresh or dry; lift roots in autumn |
| USES | |
| *Medicinally* | See below |
| *In the home* | As a dye |

Woad is probably best known as a dye. It is said that it was woad that the Britons painted their bodies with in order to terrify any marauding intruders; the Romans couldn't have been particularly put off by it, though, because they successfully invaded and settled here. Another, more practical, reason for painting the body with woad is because it has good antiseptic properties – any battle wounds inflicted by the enemy would heal more quickly if there was already a coating of antiseptic.

Until the 1630s, when indigo was imported from the tropics, woad was the best blue dye available for fabrics. Its use died out but in recent years it has experienced a bit of a come-back, with people revitalising many of the more 'traditional' crafts.

From a medicinal perspective, there are conflicting points of view as to whether woad is safe to use internally for various ailments. Probably the best advice is to leave it to the professionals to decide. Woad appears to have medicinal potential, irrespective of differing views. In 2006, research scientists at the University of Bologna in Italy demonstrated that woad, being a member of the Brassicaceae family – the same family to which broccoli belongs – can produce surprising amounts of the cancer-fighting biochemical glucobrassicin (GBS). We must wait and see if this proves to be worthy of further research.

### *Lavandula angustifolia*
Common names: Lavender, English lavender

| | |
|---|---|
| Type of plant/Hardiness | Evergreen shrub/H4 – hardy |
| Height and spread | Up to 70cm/70cm, depending on cultivar |
| Best position | Sun |
| Soil | Well drained |
| Method(s) of propagation | By semi-hardwood cuttings |

| Part of plant used | Flowers |
| --- | --- |
| Harvest | Pick flowers as they begin to open to use fresh or to dry |

USES

| *Medicinally* | Externally: for burns; skin conditions; insect bites |
| --- | --- |
| | Internally: to aid relaxation; for digestive disorders |
| *Cosmetically* | In skin and bathing preparations; in perfume |
| *In the home* | As an insect repellent; in pot pourri; in a clothes rinse |

Lavender must be one of the most well-known and well-loved of all herbs and consequently has been written about extensively, so my offering here is a mere bagatelle.

I wouldn't be without lavender in my garden: for a short time I lived in a flat and the only 'garden' I had was a window box – you can no doubt guess what it was planted with! Its worth is universal, from being used in medicinal and cosmetic preparations, through home and culinary applications, to being a beautiful garden plant, beloved by bees. What more could one ask for?

Lavender is native to dry, rocky regions of the Mediterranean. Its name comes from the Latin *lavare,* meaning to wash, and the Romans used lavender to scent their bath water. Indeed it is thought that it was the Romans who brought lavender to our shores, although the first written reference to it does not appear until a manuscript of 1265. Since then, lavender, particularly *Lavandula angustifolia*, has been grown in Britain, ranging from the odd specimen in a back garden to acres of fields for commercial production, for example in Sussex, my home county.

### *Matricaria recutita*
Common name: German chamomile

| | |
|---|---|
| Type of plant/Hardiness | Annual/H4 – hardy |
| Height and spread | Up to 60cm/30cm |
| Best position | Sun |
| Soil | Well drained. Neutral to slightly acid conditions |
| Method(s) of propagation | By seed sown in autumn or spring |
| Part of plant used | Leaves, roots |
| Harvest | Pick flowers when just fully open to use fresh or to freeze |
| USES | |
| *Medicinally* | Externally: for sore skin |
| | Internally: to aid relaxation; for digestive disorders |
| *Cosmetically* | In shampoo to lighten the hair |
| *In the home* | As an insect repellent. As a dye |

German chamomile is used in very much the same way as Roman chamomile and, indeed, they are pretty much interchangeable. The fragrance of German chamomile is a little less pronounced than the Roman one, and it is also a little less bitter, which makes it a more palatable ingredient in tisanes.

### *Melissa officinalis*
Common name: Lemon balm

| | |
|---|---|
| Type of plant/Hardiness | Perennial/H4 – hardy |
| Height and spread | Up to 60cm/75cm – but see below |

| | |
|---|---|
| Best position | Sun. Dappled shade is tolerated |
| Soil | Moisture retentive, but not waterlogged |
| Method(s) of propagation | By seed sown in spring; by softwood cuttings; by division in spring or autumn |
| Part of plant used | Leaves |
| Harvest | Pick leaves just before flowers appear to use fresh or to dry |
| USES | |
| *Medicinally* | Externally: for insect bites; cold sores Internally: to relieve headaches; for digestive disorders; to cheer you up! |
| *In the home* | In pot pourri |

Lemon balm is native to southern Europe and has been cultivated for over 2,000 years: it was brought to Britain by the Romans. Melissa is the Greek word for honey bee and the herb has long been associated with apiculture. Not only is it a rich source of nectar, but Virgil (70–19 BCE) notes that lemon balm induces swarming, and in the sixteenth century the herbalist John Gerard wrote that: 'The hives of bees being rubbed with the leaves of balm causeth the bees to keep together and causeth others to come with them.'

Lemon balm was the key ingredient in what was known as 'Carmelite Water', a 'tonic-cum-eau de toilette' in much the same vein as Queen of Hungary Water (see page 75). Most sources date its origins to the fourteenth century, when it was made at the Abbaye St Juste by the Carmelite incumbents – hence its name. Mixed with various other herbs, spices and alcohol it served both to disguise body odour and as a stimulating tonic to drink. A version of it, called *Eau de Melisse*, is still made in France today.

If the lemon balm plant likes where you have planted it, it will make itself at home to the point of sprawling over its allotted space – a bit like my son, when he was a teenager, was wont to do on the settee! Keep trimming it back to remind it where it belongs. As well as the green-leaved variety there is a variegated form which has splashes of yellow, and sometimes white, on the leaves; it is slightly (but only slightly) less invasive than the all-green variety.

### *Mentha spicata*

Common names: Spearmint, garden mint

| | |
|---|---|
| Type of plant/Hardiness | Perennial/H4 – hardy |
| Height and spread | Up to 60cm/indefinite |
| Best position | Sun or partial shade |
| Soil | Rich, moisture retentive, but not waterlogged |
| Method(s) of propagation | By division in spring or autumn; by cuttings placed in water during growing season |
| Part of plant used | Leaves |
| Harvest | Gather leaves as required to use fresh or to dry |
| USES | |
| *Medicinally* | Internally: for colic; wind; and indigestion |
| *Cosmetically* | In toothpastes |
| *In the home* | In pot pourri |

Who hasn't heard of mint? The majority of us habitually have mint sauce with our roast lamb; indeed, spearmint is the mint that is used most often in cooking. But it also finds its way into other preparations, such as toothpaste (although this is often peppermint – see below), chewing gum, and the mint tea that many of us take as a digestif.

The major problem with growing mint is that once you have it in your garden you can't get rid of it. Let it loose and it will bully its way out of its allocated space and will grow roughshod over lesser vegetation. I have found the best way to grow it is in a container. Although it is a perennial and will come back every year, I tend to replace it every other year simply because it tends to sulk after a while because you won't let it have its rein. Given that it is so easy to propagate – simply snip a stem off and place it in water and roots will soon begin to emerge – you can afford to forfeit the parent plant.

### *Mentha pulegium*
Common name: Pennyroyal

| | |
|---|---|
| Type of plant/Hardiness | Perennial/H4 – hardy |
| Height and spread | 20cm/50cm |
| Best position | Sun or partial shade |
| Soil | Damp, slightly acid |
| Method(s) of propagation | By seed sown in spring; by division in spring or autumn; by cuttings placed in water any time during the growing season |
| Part of plant used | Leaves |
| Harvest | Pick leaves as required and to dry |
| USES | |
| *Medicinally* | Externally: for skin irritations<br>Internally: for indigestion and colic |
| *Cosmetically* | In soaps |

| *In the home* | As a rodent and insect repellent; in pot pourri |

Like many other members of the mint family, pennyroyal is a good remedy for indigestion; however, too much of it can be far from beneficial since an excess of the oil can lead to organ failure.

Where Pennyroyal really comes into its own is as an insect, and particularly flea, repellent. For centuries it was used as a strewing herb and it was rubbed on dogs and other domestic animals to keep fleas at bay: indeed, its species name, *pulegium*, comes from the Latin *pulex*, meaning flea. Pennyroyal enjoys varying status depending on where in the world it is growing: in parts of Europe it is a protected species, whereas in some countries, notably parts of Australia, it is subject to statutory control as a weed.

### *Mentha* x *piperata*
Common name: Peppermint

| | |
|---|---|
| Type of plant/Hardiness | Perennial/H4 – hardy |
| Height and spread | 60cm/Indefinite |
| Best position | Sun or partial shade |
| Soil | Moisture retentive but not waterlogged |
| Method(s) of propagation | By division in spring or autumn; by cuttings placed in water any time during the growing season |
| Part of plant used | Leaves |
| Harvest | Pick leaves as required and to dry |

USES

| | |
|---|---|
| *Medicinally* | Externally: as a rub or steam inhalation to relieve cough and cold symptoms |
| | Internally: for indigestion; colic; flatulence; and nausea |
| *Cosmetically* | In oral hygiene preparations |
| *In the home* | In pot pourri; as a rodent repellent |

I would wager that the vast majority of us come across peppermint every day without really taking notice of it. The reason I say this is that most toothpastes which taste of mint do, in fact, owe their flavour to peppermint. It is possible that nowadays synthetic flavourings are used in some; nevertheless the original minty taste comes from the oil of *Mentha* x *piperata*. What we humans find refreshing and flavourful, other creatures, especially rodents, find repulsive. In the past many farmers grew a defensive cordon of peppermint around their granaries to keep rats and mice at bay.

### *Ocimum basilicum*
Common names: Basil, sweet basil

| | |
|---|---|
| Type of plant/Hardiness | Annual/H1b Heated greenhouse – subtropical |
| Height and spread | 60cm/30cm |
| Best position | Sun |
| Soil | Light, well drained |
| Method(s) of propagation | By seed sown in spring at 13°C minimum |
| Part of plant used | Whole plant, leaves |
| Harvest | Gather whole plants just before flowering; pick leaves as required and to dry |

USES

| | |
|---|---|
| *Medicinally* | Externally: for stings and bites; for skin infections; acne |
| | Internally: for colds and flu; digestion; nausea; low spirits |
| *In the home* | As an insect repellent |

Most of us have come across basil in pesto or as an accompaniment to tomatoes, either fresh or in a sauce. Perhaps not everyone knows it as a medicinal herb though. It belongs to the mint family and, like many of its cousins, is a good aid to digestion. Apparently, it is also an excellent mood enhancer – a cup of basil tisane will cheer you up and help relieve anxiety.

Basil is also an excellent insect repellent: the juice of the leaves will repel mosquitoes, and a pot of basil in the kitchen will deter those pesky flies.

### *Ocimum tenuiflorum*
Common names: Holy basil, sacred basil

| | |
|---|---|
| Type of plant/Hardiness | Short-lived perennial/H1b Heated greenhouse – subtropical |
| Height and spread | 60cm/30cm |
| Best position | Sun |
| Soil | Light, well drained |
| Method(s) of propagation | By seed sown in spring – minimum 13°C |
| Part of plant used | Flowers and leaves |
| Harvest | Pick leaves as required and to dry |
| USES | |
| *Medicinally* | Externally: for stings and bites; for skin infections |

|  | Internally: flowers for coughs and colds; leaves for nausea, diarrhoea and flatulence |
| *In the home* | As an insect repellent |

*Ocimum tenuiflorum* is regarded as sacred in Hinduism, hence its common name of holy or sacred basil. The woody stems are used to make rosary beads but this basil's use goes beyond the contemplative. It is also a valuable medicinal herb, bringing relief for a range of symptoms, from skin infections to flatulence.

Although it is technically a perennial herb, outside its native subtropical zone it is more usually grown as an annual in greenhouse conditions.

### *Origanum majorana*
Common name: Sweet marjoram

| Type of plant/Hardiness | Evergreen perennial/H3 – half hardy |
| Height and spread | 60cm/30cm |
| Best position | Sun |
| Soil | Light, well drained |
| Method(s) of propagation | By seed sown in spring or autumn – minimum 10–13°C; by basal cuttings in spring; by division in spring |
| Part of plant used | Flowers and leaves |
| Harvest | Pick leaves and flowers as required and to dry |
| USES | |
| *Medicinally* | Externally: for bronchial congestion, muscular pain, stiff joints |

| | Internally: for bronchial complaints; headaches; anxiety |
|---|---|
| *Cosmetically* | In soaps and shampoo |
| *In the home* | In pot pourri; as an insect repellent |

So when is marjoram oregano, and vice versa? My understanding is that marjoram (or sweet marjoram) refers to *Origanum majorana* and oregano is *Origanum vulgare*. I make this distinction because *O. majorana* is less hardy than *O. vulgare*. *O. majorana* won't cope with temperatures below freezing so I tend to grow it as an annual.

Like its cousin *Origanum vulgare*, sweet marjoram is nowadays mostly used in the kitchen – both are indispensable in Italian and other Mediterranean dishes. They can also be employed in cosmetic and household preparations, as well as for making a soothing tisane to alleviate mild headaches and anxiety.

### *Origanum vulgare*
Common name: Oregano

| | |
|---|---|
| Type of plant/Hardiness | Evergreen perennial/H4 – hardy |
| Height and spread | 60cm/30cm |
| Best position | Sun |
| Soil | Light, well drained |
| Method(s) of propagation | By seed sown in spring or autumn – minimum 10–13°C; by basal cuttings in spring; by division in spring |
| Part of plant used | Flowers and leaves |
| Harvest | Pick leaves and flowers as required and to dry |

USES
*Medicinally*              Externally: for bronchial congestion;
                          muscular pain; stiff joints
                          Internally: for bronchial complaints;
                          headaches and anxiety; indigestion
*Cosmetically*            In soaps and shampoo
*In the home*             In pot pourri; as an insect repellent

There always seems to be confusion between oregano and marjoram, the common names at least apparently being interchangeable; the Latin genus name is the same for both, however, namely *Origanum*.

Personally, I use the name marjoram for the herb known as sweet marjoram, whose Latin name is *Origanum majorana*, and use the name oregano for *O. vulgare*. *O. vulgare* is hardier than *O. majorana* and can withstand temperatures below freezing.

I wouldn't be without either oregano or marjoram growing in my garden, not only because both herbs are so useful, but also because, if some are left to flower, they attract so many bees. The flowers produce nectar which has a very high sugar content – up to 80 per cent. Although attractive to bees, many other insects are repelled by it, so oregano also makes a good bug deterrent.

All species of *Origanum* appear to originate from the Mediterranean; nowadays, however, many species can be found growing wild in various places, including the chalk downs of Britain. In addition to this there are many decorative forms of oregano with different coloured leaves or flowers – all of them can be used, but to my mind the straightforward *Origanum vulgare* is still the best.

### *Pelargonium capitatum*
Common name: Rose-scented geranium

| | |
|---|---|
| Type of plant/Hardiness | Evergreen perennial/H1c – warm temperate |
| Height and spread | Up to 90cm/Up to 1.5m |
| Best position | Sun |
| Soil | Well drained, neutral to alkaline |
| Method(s) of propagation | By softwood cuttings throughout the growing season |
| Part of plant used | Leaves and flowers |
| Harvest | Pick leaves and flowers as required |
| USES | |
| *Medicinally* | Externally: for dry and cracked skin |
| *Cosmetically* | In bath preparations |
| *In the home* | In pot pourri |

There are, literally, hundreds of different species and varieties of *Pelargonium*. Many, like *P. capitatum*, have fragrant leaves from which oil is extracted: this is the geranium (or often rose geranium) oil which is used in cosmetic and some medicinal preparations. The name geranium is properly applied to the related, hardy, perennial genus, but old habits die hard and the misnomer lingers.

Native to South Africa the first *Pelargonium* (*P.triste*) was introduced to Britain in the seventeenth century by John Tradescant the Elder. He bought seeds, or possibly a plant, from Rene Morin, one of the greatest French nurserymen of his time, who, in 1621, published one of the first plant catalogues in the world, the *Catalogus plantarum horti Renati Morini*.

Exactly when 'our' *Pelargonium* was first seen in Britain is not recorded, but being a species it is likely that it followed soon after the first found its way here.

### *Petroselinum crispum*
Common name: Parsley

| | |
|---|---|
| Type of plant/Hardiness | Biennial/H4 – hardy |
| Height and spread | 45cm/45cm |
| Best position | Sun or partial shade |
| Soil | Deep, fertile |
| Method(s) of propagation | By seed, sown outdoors in spring or autumn |
| Part of plant used | Roots, seeds and leaves |
| Harvest | Lift roots in autumn of first year, or spring of second year; collect seeds when ripe; pick leaves as required and to dry |

USES
| | |
|---|---|
| *Medicinally* | Externally: to ease insect bites |
| | Internally: to aid digestion; as a mild diuretic; to ease anxiety |
| *Cosmetically* | In shampoos to combat dandruff |

Parsley is arguably the most well-known herb in the Western world. It is a native of central and southern Europe but is now widely grown in its various forms throughout the world. It carries with it some superstitious beliefs, one being that only a pregnant woman or a witch can grow it – well I'm certainly not pregnant!

The most common types are the curly leaved parsley (*Petroselinum crispum*) and the flat leaved, French or Italian parsley (*Petroselinum crispum* var. *Neapolitanum*). They both require the same cultivation, namely a good, rich soil which must not be acid. They also require regular watering. Although parsley is a biennial, most people grow it as an annual because in its second year it will run to seed very quickly. If you want leaves over the dormant season, sow seed in the autumn and protect the plants with a cloche or horticultural fleece over winter.

### *Pimpinella anisum*
Common name: Aniseed

| | |
|---|---|
| Type of plant/Hardiness | Annual/H3 – half hardy |
| Height and spread | 30–90cm/30cm |
| Best position | Sun |
| Soil | Rich, well drained |
| Method(s) of propagation | By seed when ripe |
| Part of plant used | Leaves, seeds |
| Harvest | Gather leaves in summer; collect seeds as they ripen |
| USES | |
| *Medicinally* | Externally: as a chest rub |
| | Internally: for coughs and other bronchial problems; as a digestive aid |
| *In the home* | To attract mice to traps – so you can deal with them as you see fit! |

Aniseed is used extensively for culinary purposes: it can be found in curry powder, in confectionery and is the basis for anise-flavoured drinks such as *pastis* and *ouzo* – no Greek holiday is complete without bringing a bottle of the latter home!

Aniseed has also been used medicinally for centuries: it is mentioned by both Dioscorides (40–90 BCE) and Pliny (23–79 BCE) and, having found its way to England, is mentioned as having been used as a breath freshener and digestive aid in herbals dating from the early 1500s.

*Pimpinella* is a member of the Apiaceae family, which has characteristic umbels of flowers, many of which are white. You should take extra care with these and be certain to identify them accurately because not only does the family include benign herbs such as *Myrrhis odorata* (sweet Cicely) and *Daucus carota* (wild carrot), but also highly poisonous ones, like the deadly *Conium maculatum* (hemlock). If you are in any doubt at all, leave well alone.

### Plantago major

| | |
|---|---|
| Common name: Plantain | |
| Type of plant/hardiness | Perennial/H4 – hardy |
| Height and spread | 40cm/40cm |
| Best position | Sun |
| Soil | Well drained |
| Method(s) of propagation | By seed in autumn or spring |
| Part of plant used | Leaves |
| Harvest | Cut leaves as required before the plant flowers |
| USES | |
| *Medicinally* | Externally: for wounds; bites; shingles; haemorrhoids |
| | Internally: for diarrhoea; cystitis; catarrh; bronchitis |

You may be wondering why anyone would actually want to cultivate plantain – it is such an endemic plant that you really wouldn't need to look very far before you found one, which is probably Mother Nature's way of providing a panacea for numerous and varied complaints. It's been used for centuries for all manner of ills and not just in humans. Apparently it will cure the madness of dogs, toads will eat plantain leaves to neutralise poison if bitten by a spider, and a dog which had been bitten by a rattlesnake was reputedly cured after an application of plantain juice.

### *Prunella vulgaris*
Common names: Self-heal, carpenter's herb

| | |
|---|---|
| Type of plant/hardiness | Perennial/H4 – hardy |
| Height and spread | 50cm/indefinite |
| Best position | Sun or partial shade |
| Soil | Well drained, moisture retentive |
| Method(s) of propagation | By seed sown in autumn or spring; by division in spring |
| Part of plant used | Leaves, stems and flowers |
| Harvest | Cut when in flower |
| USES | |
| *Medicinally* | Externally: for cuts; grazes; and minor wounds and injuries including bleeding haemorrhoids |
| | Internally: for internal bleeding; sore throats |

In the seventeenth century Nicholas Culpepper explained why *Prunella vulgaris* is called self-heal: 'When you are hurt, you may heal yourself.' Simple! And a century before, Gerard wrote: 'There is not a better wounde herbe in the world ... being only bruised and wrought with the point of a knife upon a trencher [plate] ... will be brought into the form of a salve, which will heal any green [fresh] wound even in the first intention [application], after a very wonderful manner.' Indeed, its other common name of carpenter's herb indicates that it was traditionally used for cut and bruised fingers and hands.

Although *Prunella vulgaris* has attractive purple flowers – like many other members of the Lamiaceae family, including lavender – you may not want to grow it deliberately in your herbaceous border: it can be invasive to the point of being an utter nuisance. It will probably crop up unbidden in your lawn, anyway, but if you do want to cultivate it, confine it to a 'wilder' part of the garden.

### *Rosa gallica* var. *officinalis*
Common name: Apothecary's rose

| | |
|---|---|
| Type of plant/hardiness | Shrub/H4 – hardy |
| Height and spread | 80cm/1m |
| Best position | Sun |
| Soil | Well drained, moisture retentive. Can tolerate slightly acid conditions and clay |
| Method(s) of propagation | By hardwood cuttings in autumn |
| Part of plant used | Flower buds, petals |
| Harvest | Pick buds when colour begins to show; collect petals when flowers first open |
| USES | |
| *Medicinally* | Externally: for skin problems and minor injuries |
| | Internally: for colds; diarrhoea; sore throats |
| *Cosmetically* | In bath and skin-care products |
| *In the home* | In pot pourri |

Gertrude Stein (the early twentieth-century novelist and poet) famously wrote in a non-herbal context: 'A rose, is a rose, is a rose.' But, herbally speaking, roses are not all the same. There are the big, blousy, old-fashioned blossoms; prim, hybrid teas; multi-bloomed floribundas; repeat-flowering, English roses. But the one that is traditionally associated with herbal applications is the Apothecary's rose – *Rosa gallica* var. *officinalis*. This is the rose that has very fragrant, semi-double, crimson flowers, which have been used for centuries for all sorts of applications from treating skin irritations to fragrancing a room.

It is rose oil that is nearly always used in commercial products. But bearing in mind it takes approximately 2 million flowers to make 900g of oil it is no wonder that the oil is so highly prized – and so expensive!

### *Rosmarinus officinalis*
Common name: Rosemary

| | |
|---|---|
| Type of plant/hardiness | Evergreen shrub/H4 – hardy |
| Height and spread | 90cm/60m |
| Best position | Sun |
| Soil | Well drained |
| Method(s) of propagation | By semi-ripe cuttings; by layering |
| Part of plant used | Leaves, flowering stems |
| Harvest | Pick flowering stems in spring; pick leaves as required |

USES
*Medicinally*          Externally: for wounds and muscular injuries

|              |                                                      |
|--------------|------------------------------------------------------|
|              | Internally: for apathy and anxiety; tension headaches; as a memory enhancer |
| *Cosmetically* | In shampoos, skin-care and bath products             |
| *In the home*  | In pot pourri; as an insect repellent                |

Rosemary is native to scrubby, coastal regions of the Mediterranean – its Latin name, *Rosmarinus*, means 'dew of the sea'. It also grows abundantly inland: during the sixteenth century, the French gardener Olivier de Serres noted that in Provence rosemary was so abundant that its woody stems were used as fuel in bread ovens. Rosemary is a symbol of fidelity and remembrance – Sir Thomas More (1478–1535) wrote: 'As for Rosemarine, I let it run all over my garden walls, not only because my bees love it, but because 'tis the herb sacred to remembrance, and, therefore, to friendship.'

There are a number of varieties of rosemary available, ranging from the 'straight-laced' sounding 'Miss Jessop's Upright' to the more frivolous sounding 'Majorca Pink'; however, the rosemary that is most widely used in herbal preparations is the well-known *Rosmarinus officinalis*.

### *Ruta graveoloens*
Common name: Rue

|                        |                                                      |
|------------------------|------------------------------------------------------|
| Type of plant/hardiness | Evergreen subshrub/H4 – hardy                        |
| Height and spread      | 60cm/45m                                             |
| Best position          | Sun                                                  |
| Soil                   | Well drained; can withstand slightly alkaline conditions |

| | |
|---|---|
| Method(s) of propagation | By seed sown in spring; by semi-ripe cuttings |
| Part of plant used | Leaves |
| Harvest | Pick leaves in spring and summer – but see warning below |
| USES | |
| *Medicinally* | Externally: for sprains and bruising – but see warning below |
| *In the home* | As an insect repellent |
| ☠ BEWARE ☠ | Skin irritant – can cause severe blistering in sunlight |

Although rue has a long history of use as a medicinal remedy, it should be used with extreme caution because it is highly toxic in large amounts and can cause severe skin irritation.

The only use I put rue to is as a very effective insect repellent, either fresh in a vase or in 'Vinegar of the Four Thieves' – see page 107.

### *Salvia officinalis*
Common names: Sage, garden sage, common sage

| | |
|---|---|
| Type of plant/hardiness | Evergreen subshrub/H4 – hardy |
| Height and spread | 60cm/45m |
| Best position | Sun |
| Soil | Well drained |
| Method(s) of propagation | By seed sown in spring; by softwood cuttings in spring; by semi-ripe cuttings in summer |
| Part of plant used | Leaves |
| Harvest | Pick leaves as required to use fresh and to dry |

USES

| | |
|---|---|
| *Medicinally* | Externally: for insect bites; mouth and skin infections; minor cuts and grazes<br>Internally: for indigestion; flatulence; night sweats; to aid mental capacity |
| *Cosmetically* | In toothpaste and skin preparations |
| *In the home* | As an insect repellent |

Sage has always been a highly prized medicinal herb – its name is testament to this: the Genus name '*Salvia*' is said to be derived from the Latin *salvere* meaning to save or heal, and the Species name '*officinalis*' comes from the Latin word *opificina* meaning a herb store or pharmacy.

An Arabic proverb claims that: 'He who has sage in his garden will not die.' Whether sage will guarantee your immortality is questionable but it has long been held that it will improve your memory and mental capacity. Gerard, in his *Herbal* of 1597, tells us that: 'Sage is singularly good for the head and brain, it quickeneth the senses and memory …' Recent research appears to confirm Gerard's assertions: a study at The Medicinal Plant Research Centre (a research partnership between the Universities of Newcastle, Northumbria and Durham) showed that oil derived from sage did indeed improve the memory of a group of adults. Now, where did I leave my cup of sage tea?

*Salvia officinalis* is the best known sage but there are other varieties, notably gold sage (*Salvia officinalis* 'Icterina') and purple sage (*Salvia officinalis* Purpurascens Group). Indeed, some herbalists regard purple sage as more potent than the ordinary garden sage.

**Sambucus nigra**
Common name: Elder

| | |
|---|---|
| Type of plant/hardiness | Deciduous shrub or tree/H4 – hardy |
| Height and spread | 6m/3m |
| Best position | Sun or partial shade |
| Soil | Rich, moist. Can tolerate alkaline conditions |
| Method(s) of propagation | By softwood cuttings in early summer; by hardwood cuttings in winter |
| Part of plant used | Flowers, leaves and fruit |
| Harvest | Gather open flowers in late spring and early summer as required to use fresh and to dry; pick leaves as required; pick ripe berries in autumn |
| USES | |
| *Medicinally* | Externally: flowers – for inflamed or chapped hands, chilblains, minor burns and scalds |
| | Leaves – for bruises and sprains |
| | Internally: flowers – for coughs and colds; as a mouthwash |
| | Berries – in a syrup for coughs and colds; as a laxative |
| *Cosmetically* | Flowers – in skin lotions |
| *In the home* | As a dye, especially the berries |
| ☠ BEWARE ☠ | Leaves and raw berries can be extremely harmful if eaten. (I can't imagine that you'd want to eat a leaf though – the fetid smell would be enough to put anyone off.) |

Elder is a ubiquitous hedgerow plant: walk along any country lane and you are bound to come across one sooner or later. In late spring and early summer the frothy white flowers clothe the shrub, followed by a dripping harvest of globose, almost black, berries in the autumn. Both flowers and berries are popularly used in the kitchen to make, variously, cordials, jams and syrups, but the flowers and berries can also be used in medicinal preparations. The leaves, on the other hand, are rarely used nowadays, although at one time they were the key ingredient in a green ointment known as *unguentum sambuci viride* which was used to treat bruises and sprains.

Elder is surrounded by manifold superstitions and folklore – from having to ask permission of the Elder Mother before you chop down a tree, to pinning elder leaves on your front door on the last day of April to prevent witches from entering. A more plausible saying is that summer only truly begins when elderflower is in blossom, and ends when the berries are ripe on the bush.

### *Saponaria officinalis*
Common names: Soapwort, bouncing Bet

| | |
|---|---|
| Type of plant/hardiness | Perennial/H4 – hardy |
| Height and spread | 60cm/60cm |
| Best position | Sun or partial shade |
| Soil | Well drained, moist, neutral to alkaline |
| Method(s) of propagation | By seed sown in spring or autumn; by division in spring |
| Part of plant used | Leafy stems and rhizomes |
| Harvest | Pick leafy stems in summer; lift rhizomes in late autumn to dry |

USES
*Cosmetically*            In shampoo

| *In the home* | As a mild household cleaner |

*Saponaria officinalis* used to be used extensively as a medicinal expectorant; however, due to the excessive irritant effect on the gut it is rarely used today. Where it does come into its own, though, is as a mild cleanser. Both its Latin and common names are an indication of this: *sapo* is Latin for soap, and soapwort is obvious!

It is a pretty plant to have in the garden, although it can be a little invasive if you don't keep an eye on it.

A word of warning if you do plant it in your garden: it is poisonous to fish, so don't allow either roots or leaves to come into contact with pond water.

### *Satureja montana*
Common names: Winter savory, bean herb

| | |
|---|---|
| Type of plant/hardiness | Semi-evergreen subshrub/H4 – hardy |
| Height and spread | 20cm/20cm |
| Best position | Sun |
| Soil | Well drained, neutral to alkaline |
| Method(s) of propagation | By seed sown in spring; by division in autumn or spring; by semi-ripe cuttings in summer |
| Part of plant used | Leaves |
| Harvest | Pick leaves as required to use fresh and to dry |
| USES | |
| *Medicinally* | Externally: for insect bites and stings Internally: for indigestion; flatulence |

There are two types of savory in widespread cultivation: the perennial subshrub, *Satureja montana,* known as winter savory, and the annual, *Satureja hortensis*, known as summer savory. Both share the same properties and are used in the same way – the only difference is that summer savory has to be sown anew each spring.

Both are valued for their ability to moderate flatulence. One of the common names which they both share is bean herb – as we all know, beans can produce excess wind, so a helping of savory, either freshly chopped and sprinkled on the beans, or taken in a tisane afterwards will help to reduce any discomfort.

### *Stachys officinalis*

Common names: Betony, woundwort, all-heal

| | |
|---|---|
| Type of plant/hardiness | Perennial/H4 – hardy |
| Height and spread | Up to 60cm/45cm |
| Best position | Sun or partial shade |
| Soil | Well drained, moisture retentive |
| Method(s) of propagation | By seed sown in autumn or spring; by division in spring |
| Part of plant used | Whole plant |
| Harvest | Cut whole plant in summer to use fresh and to dry |
| USES | |
| *Medicinally* | Externally: for all manner of wounds and bruises |
| | Internally: for nervous headaches and anxiety |

*Stachys officinalis* has long been recognised as a healing herb. Gerard in his *Herbal* of 1597 gives us an insight as to how it is best used: 'The leaves hereof … applied unto greene [fresh] wounds in manner of a pultesse (poultice), heale them in short time, and in such absolute manner, that it is hard for any that have not had the experience thereof to believe.' Nowadays modern dressings have taken the place of such poultices, but the efficacy of woundwort is worth remembering for minor cuts and grazes.

On a non-medicinal note, *Stachys officinalis*, along with its cousin, the non-herbal *Stachys byzantina*, make excellent garden plants: the former has spikes of pink flowers, beloved by bees; the latter has downy, grey leaves, which gives it its common name of lamb's ears.

### *Symphytum officinale*
Common names: Comfrey, knitbone

| | |
|---|---|
| Type of plant/hardiness | Perennial/H4 – hardy |
| Height and spread | Up to 1.2m/60cm |
| Best position | Sun or partial shade |
| Soil | Moisture retentive |
| Method(s) of propagation | By seed sown in autumn or spring; by division in spring or autumn |
| Part of plant used | Leaves, roots |
| Harvest | Pick leaves in early summer before flowering to dry; lift roots over winter |

USES
*Medicinally* — Externally: for fractures; skin conditions; sprains; cuts

☠ BEWARE ☠ — Do not take internally – may contain carcinogenic compounds
The bristly leaves may cause skin irritation

Once used internally as a remedy for arthritis, *Symphytum*

*officinale* has since been banned by a number of countries because of the increased risk of liver cancer. However, it has been used even longer, and safely, for the external treatment of a number of skin conditions, cuts, sprains and bruises.

Where it really comes into its own, though, is as a treatment for fractures. The Romans called *Symphytum officinale 'conferva'* meaning 'joining together' (from which we get one of its common names, comfrey; its other common name is knitbone) so it has a long and established pedigree as a herb known for its fracture-healing properties. If you are unfortunate enough to fracture a bone which would not normally be set in plaster, such as a toe, try a poultice made with puréed comfrey leaves – it certainly won't do any harm.

Beware if you plant *Symphytum officinale* in your garden, though – it has a habit of outgrowing its allotted space and becoming a bit of an annoyance.

### *Tanacetum parthenium*
Common name: Feverfew

| | |
|---|---|
| Type of plant/hardiness | Short-lived perennial/H4 – hardy |
| Height and spread | Up to 60cm/45cm |
| Best position | Sun |
| Soil | Very well drained |
| Method(s) of propagation | By seed sown at 10–13°C in spring; by division in spring or autumn; by basal cuttings in spring; by semi-ripe cuttings in summer |
| Part of plant used | Whole plant, leaves |
| Harvest | Cut whole plants when flowering; pick leaves as required to dry |

USES

| | |
|---|---|
| *Medicinally* | Externally: for headaches; insect bites; bruising |
| | Internally: for migraine headaches; rheumatic and arthritic complaints; fevers |
| *In the home* | As an insect repellent |
| ☠ BEWARE ☠ | Handling the leaves may cause dermatitis; eating the leaves may cause mouth ulcers |

Feverfew has long been held to be efficacious at easing the symptoms of migraine headaches, although there is no conclusive scientific evidence that this is the case. Nevertheless, some migraine sufferers swear by its capacity to alleviate the symptoms.

What there is little divergence of opinion about is that feverfew is a highly efficient insect repellent.

### *Tanacetum vulgare*
Common name: Tansy

| | |
|---|---|
| Type of plant/hardiness | Perennial/H4 – hardy |
| Height and spread | Up to 60cm/45cm |
| Best position | Sun |
| Soil | Very well drained |
| Method(s) of propagation | By seed sown at 10–13°C in spring; by division in spring or autumn; by basal cuttings in spring; by semi-ripe cuttings in summer |
| Part of plant used | Whole plant |
| Harvest | Cut whole plants when flowering |

USES

| | |
|---|---|
| *In the home* | As an insect repellent; as a dye |
| ☙ BEWARE ☙ | Do not use medicinally – the essential oil is highly toxic. Wash your hands after handling |

*Tanacetum vulgare* (tansy) was once used as a medicinal herb but we now know that it can be highly toxic. It should be restricted to household use, where, as an insect repellent, it is unsurpassed. It was used as a strewing herb to deter fleas and lice, and fresh leaves were also rubbed into pets' coats to repel fleas. Before refrigeration, tansy would have been placed around meats and other food to discourage flies – and, of course, it is still effective today if you want to keep flies out of the kitchen.

It is also possible to extract dyes from *Tanacetum vulgare* – the leaves produce green, and a rather murky yellow can be gained from the flowers.

### *Thymus vulgaris*
Common names: Thyme, common thyme

| | |
|---|---|
| Type of plant/hardiness | Shrub/H4 – hardy |
| Height and spread | 30cm/40cm |
| Best position | Sun |
| Soil | Well drained, neutral to alkaline |
| Method(s) of propagation | By seed sown in spring; by division in spring; by semi-ripe cuttings in summer; by layering |
| Part of plant used | Whole plant |
| Harvest | Cut whole plants and flowering tips when flowering begins to use fresh or to dry |

USES

| | |
|---|---|
| *Medicinally* | Externally: as an antiseptic; for fungal infections; as a mouthwash |
| | Internally: for coughs; indigestion; diarrhoea |
| *Cosmetically* | In shampoo and bath preparations |
| *In the home* | As an insect repellent; in pot pourri |

According to the Royal Horticultural Society there are about 350 species of thyme but the one which interests us is *Thymus vulgaris*, the common thyme, which many people say was introduced to Britain by the Romans.

Thyme has been used for millennia to fight infection: the Sumerians were using it as such circa 3000 BCE; in the first millennium CE, the Emperor Charlemagne ordered that it should be grown in all his gardens; and in Britain it figured in Gerard's Herbal of 1597. Faith in the herb as an antiseptic is not misplaced because one of the active constituents of thyme is *thymol,* a powerful antibacterial and antiseptic compound.

Some say that the name thyme was derived from the Greek *thumos* meaning 'courage' or 'passion' and, indeed, in the Middle Ages, ladies gave their knights a sprig of thyme or a cloth 'favour' embroidered with thyme to imbue them with courage.

## *Tropaeolum majus*
Common name: Nasturtium

| | |
|---|---|
| Type of plant/hardiness | Annual/H1c – warm temperate |
| Height and spread | 3m/1.5m |
| Best position | Sun |

| | |
|---|---|
| Soil | Well drained, moisture retentive, not too rich |
| Method(s) of propagation | By seed sown in spring |
| Part of plant used | Whole plant |
| Harvest | Cut whole plants, or parts, in summer |

USES

| | |
|---|---|
| *Medicinally* | Externally: for skin conditions; minor skin abrasions |
| | Internally: for respiratory infections; catarrh |
| *Cosmetically* | As a hair rinse |

*Tropaeolum* species are native to Central and South America but found their way to Europe courtesy of the conquistadors and were very soon brought to Britain. Like almost every other 'horticultural import' at that time, *Tropaeolum* would have been introduced not for its aesthetic qualities, but for its usefulness. It was already known for its antiseptic qualities, and, significantly for the Spanish conquistadors, that it could inexplicably help prevent scurvy, the scourge of many a sailor. (The link between lack of Vitamin C and scurvy was not fully recognised until much later.)

Nowadays we tend to grow it as an ornamental summer plant, but its flowers and leaves will add a peppery, watercress-like flavour to salads – and you will be getting a boost of Vitamin C at the same time!

### *Urtica dioica*

Common names: Nettle, stinging nettle

Type of plant/hardiness  Perennial/H4 – hardy

| | |
|---|---|
| Height and spread | 1.5m/indefinite |
| Best position | Sun or partial shade |
| Soil | Rich, moist |
| Method(s) of propagation | By seed sown in autumn; by division in spring |
| Part of plant used | Whole plant, leaves and roots |
| Harvest | Cut whole plants as flowering begins to use fresh or to dry; pick leaves when very young |

USES

| | |
|---|---|
| *Medicinally* | Externally: for skin conditions; general pain relief for arthritis, gout, neuralgia and sprains |
| | Internally: as an all-round tonic; for blood disorders such as anaemia |
| *Cosmetically* | In hair rinse for dandruff |
| *In the home* | As a dye; fibres are used to make cloth and string; fly repellent |
| ☠ BEWARE ☠ | The hairs on mature leaves can 'sting', causing skin irritation |

I bet I can guess what a number of you are thinking: why on earth has she given us all this information about how to grow this weed? And I did wonder myself whether I should do so because nettles are so pervasive and abundant that we spend most of our time trying to get rid of the things.

Having said it is regarded as a weed, *Urtica dioica* is actually worth having in the garden because of its many non-horticultural uses. It has been used for centuries to help with skin conditions such as eczema, and to relieve pain associated with a number of conditions such as arthritis and gout. It is also regarded as a good all-round tonic, so much so that commercially produced nettle tea is now available.

### *Valeriana officinalis*
Common name: Valerian

| | |
|---|---|
| Type of plant/hardiness | Perennial/H4 – hardy |
| Height and spread | 1.5m/1.2m |
| Best position | Sun or partial shade |
| Soil | Moist |
| Method(s) of propagation | By seed sown in spring; by basal cuttings in spring; by division in spring or autumn |
| Part of plant used | Rhizomes and roots |
| Harvest | Lift rhizomes and roots in the second year to dry, after the leaves have died back |
| USES | |
| *Medicinally* | Externally: for minor injuries, especially to draw splinters; for skin conditions such as eczema<br>Internally: for insomnia; hyperactivity; anxiety |

Valerian's effectiveness as a sleep-inducer is confirmed by the fact that there are so many over-the-counter 'natural sleeping pills' that contain it. But it is not a newly discovered remedy: we know that it was used by Hippocrates in the fourth century BCE and it appeared in eleventh-century herbal recipes. Its on-going popularity is probably due to the fact that it is effective without being addictive, it does not react with alcohol, and it doesn't give you a 'fuzzy' head in the morning.

Be aware that valerian can be irresistible to cats. Unfortunately it is equally irresistible to mice and rats: legend has it that the Pied Piper of Hamelin lured the rats out of the city because he stuffed his pockets with valerian.

*Valeriana officinalis* should not be confused with *Centranthus ruber*, which shares the same common name of valerian. The latter is purely ornamental and has no herbal use at all.

### *Verbascum thrapsus*
Common name: Mullein – but see below

| | |
|---|---|
| Type of plant/hardiness | Biennial/H4 – hardy |
| Height and spread | Up to 2m/1m |
| Best position | Sun |
| Soil | Well drained to dry |
| Method(s) of propagation | By seed sown in late or early summer; by root cuttings in late winter |
| Part of plant used | Leaves and flowers |
| Harvest | Pick flowers in summer to use fresh or to dry; pick leaves in summer to dry |
| USES | |
| *Medicinally* | Externally: for wounds; boils; haemorrhoids; chilblains; chapped skin |
| | Internally: for coughs; bronchial complaints; tonsillitis; catarrh |
| *In the home* | As a dye |
| ☠ BEWARE ☠ | Any preparation made from the leaves should be carefully strained in order to remove the small hairs |

If you wanted to find a plant which would prove the rule that the Latin name is the best identification, then *Verbascum thrapsus* would be it. I have discovered more than fifty common names for this plant, ranging from Aaron's rod to woollen blanket herb, the most widely used being mullein.

Mullein is an imposing plant which self-seeds readily, usually just where you don't want it. Bearing in mind it is a biennial it reaches statuesque proportions amazingly quickly, rocketing skywards and leaving other, lesser plants in its wake – the Usain Bolt of the garden!

### *Zingiber officinale*
Common name: Ginger

| | |
|---|---|
| Type of plant/hardiness | Rhizomatus perennial/H1b – subtropical |
| Height and spread | 1.5m/indefinite |
| Best position | Sun with high humidity |
| Soil | Well drained, humus rich |
| Method(s) of propagation | By division in late spring |
| Part of plant used | Rhizomes |
| Harvest | Lift rhizomes during the growing season |
| USES | |
| *Medicinally* | Internally: for all kinds of nausea |

Ginger has been cultivated for its medicinal qualities for centuries. In 200 CE it was listed as a taxable commodity by the Romans and was mentioned in Chinese medical manuscripts during the later Han dynasty (206 BCE–220 CE). Although still favoured in Chinese medicine, in the Occident it is used much more widely as a culinary herb. Where it finds universal recognition, however, is as a treatment for sickness, particularly travel sickness. Although herbal remedies are not advised during pregnancy, I found that the only thing that would help me through the miserable bouts of morning sickness was a ginger biscuit – or two!

## And Finally

We've come to the end of our, albeit brief, tour around the herb garden.

I hope that by the time you read this you will be confident enough to have a go at extending the range of herbs you grow and spending many 'sweet and wholesome hours … with herbs and flowers!' You may even end up with a magnificent herb garden like my friend whom we met in the introduction.

More than that, however, I hope you use your own herbs in remedies, cosmetics and in your home. The suggestions I have put forward here can act as a springboard for you to experiment – with care, of course – with your own ideas and to develop herb-based preparations to suit your own preferences.

So, here's to many happy herb hours!

# Hardiness ratings

The following hardiness ratings are those defined by the Royal Horticultural Society and are they used in the plant entries in the Gazetteer. A big thank you goes to the RHS for allowing me to reproduce it here.

| | | | |
|---|---|---|---|
| H1a | >15°C | (USDA 13) | Heated greenhouse – tropical |
| H1b | 10 to 15°C | (USDA 12) | Heated greenhouse – subtropical |
| H1c | 5 to 10°C | (USDA 11) | Heated greenhouse – warm temperate |
| H2 | 1 to 5°C | (USDA 10b) | Tender – cool or frost-free greenhouse |
| H3 | −5 to 1°C | (USDA 9b/10a) | Half hardy – unheated greenhouse/mild winter |

| H4 | −10 to −5°C | (USDA 8b/9a) | Hardy – average winter |
|----|----|----|----|
| H5 | −15 to −10°C | (USDA 7b/8a) | Hardy – cold winter |
| H6 | −20 to −15°C | (USDA 6b/7a) | Hardy – very cold winter |
| H7 | < −20°C | (USDA 6a-1) | Very hardy |

# *List of Common Names of Plants Mentioned in the Book*

| Common Name | Latin Name |
|---|---|
| All-heal | *Stachys officinalis* |
| Alpine strawberry | *Fragaria vesca* |
| Aniseed | *Pimpinella anisum* |
| Apothecary's rose | *Rosa gallica* var. *officinalis* |
| | |
| Basil | *Ocimum basilicum* |
| Basil, sacred | *Ocimum tenuiflorum* |
| Basil, sweet | *Ocimum basilicum* |
| Bean herb | *Satureja montana* |

| Common Name | Latin Name |
| --- | --- |
| Betony | *Stachys officinalis* |
| Bloodwort | *Achillea millefolium* |
| Borage | *Borago officinalis* |
| Bouncing Bet | *Saponaria officinalis* |
| Carpenter's herb | *Prunella vulgaris* |
| Carrot, wild | *Daucus carota* |
| Chamomile, Dyer's | *Anthemis tinctoria* |
| Chamomile, German | *Matricaria recutita* |
| Chamomile, Roman | *Chamaemelum nobile* |
| Comfrey | *Symphytum officinale* |
| Common sage | *Salvia officinalis* |
| Common thyme | *Thymus vulgaris* |
| Coneflower | *Echinacea* species |
| Dill | *Anethum graveolens* |
| Dyer's chamomile | *Anthemis tinctoria* |
| Elder | *Sambucus nigra* |
| English lavender | *Lavandula angustifolia* |
| False saffron | *Carthamus tinctorius* |
| Fennel | *Foeniculum vulgare* |
| Feverfew | *Tanacetum parthenium* |
| Garden mint | *Mentha spicata* |
| Garden sage | *Salvia officinalis* |
| Garlic | *Allium sativum* |
| Geranium, rose-scented | *Pelargonium capitatum* |
| German chamomile | *Matricaria recutita* |
| Ginger | *Zingiber officinale* |
| Holy basil | *Ocimum tenuiflorum* |
| Horsetail | *Equisetum arvense* |
| Hyssop | *Hyssopus officinalis* |

## List of Common Names of Plants Mentioned in the Book

| COMMON NAME | LATIN NAME |
| --- | --- |
| Knitbone | *Symphytum officinale* |
| Lad's love | *Artemisia abrotanum* |
| Lavender | *Lavandula angustifolia* |
| Lemon balm | *Melissa officinalis* |
| Lemon verbena | *Aloysia triphylla* |
| Liquorice | *Glycyrrhiza glabra* |
| Marjoram, sweet | *Origanum majorana* |
| Marshmallow | *Althaea officinalis* |
| Mint, garden | *Mentha spicata* |
| Mullein | *Verbascum thrapsus* |
| Nasturtium | *Tropaeolum majus* |
| Nettle | *Urtica dioica* |
| Oregano | *Origanum vulgare* |
| Parsley | *Petroselinum crispum* |
| Pennyroyal | *Mentha pulegium* |
| Peppermint | *Mentha* x *piperata* |
| Plantain | *Plantago major* |
| Pot marigold | *Calendula officinalis* |
| Purple sage | *Salvia officinalis* Purpurascens Group |
| Roman chamomile | *Chamaemelum nobile* |
| Rose, Apothecary's | *Rosa gallica* var. *officinalis* |
| Rosemary | *Rosmarinus officinalis* |
| Rue | *Ruta graveoloens* |
| Sacred basil | *Ocimum tenuiflorum* |
| Safflower | *Carthamus tinctorius* |
| Saffron thistle | *Carthamus tinctorius* |
| Sage | *Salvia officinalis* |
| Sage, purple | *Salvia officinalis* Purpurascens Group |

*Home Herbal*

| COMMON NAME | LATIN NAME |
|---|---|
| St John's wort | *Hypericum perforatum* |
| Savory, winter | *Satureja montana* |
| Self-heal | *Prunella vulgaris* |
| Soapwort | *Saponaria officinalis* |
| Soldier's woundwort | *Achillea millefolium* |
| Southernwood | *Artemisia abrotanum* |
| Spearmint | *Mentha spicata* |
| Starflower | *Borago officinalis* |
| Staunchweed | *Achillea millefolium* |
| Stinging nettle | *Urtica dioica* |
| Strawberry, Alpine | *Fragaria vesca* |
| Strawberry, wild | *Fragaria vesca* |
| Sweet basil | *Ocimum basilicum* |
| Sweet marjoram | *Origanum majorana* |
| Sweet root | *Glycyrrhiza glabra* |
| Sweet woodruff | *Galium odoratum* |
| Tansy | *Tanacetum vulgare* |
| Thyme | *Thymus vulgaris* |
| Valerian | *Valeriana officinalis* |
| Wild carrot | *Daucus carota* |
| Wild strawberry | *Fragaria vesca* |
| Winter savory | *Satureja montana* |
| Witch hazel | *Hamamelis virginiana* |
| Woundwort | *Stachys officinalis* |
| Woad | *Isatis tinctoria* |
| Yarrow | *Achillea millefolium* |

# Index

# List of Herbs Mentioned in the Book and Their Uses

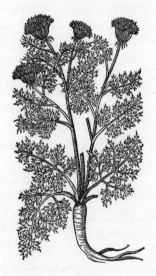

| | FIRST-AID | COSMETIC | IN THE HOME |
|---|:---:|:---:|:---:|
| *Achillea millefolium* (yarrow) | ✓ | ✓ | |
| *Allium sativum* (garlic) | ✓ | | |
| *Aloe vera* | ✓ | | |
| *Aloysia triphylla* (lemon verbena) | | ✓ | ✓ |
| *Althaea officinalis* (marshmallow) | ✓ | ✓ | |
| *Anethum graveolens* (dill) | | ✓ | |

| | First-aid | Cosmetic | In the Home |
|---|:---:|:---:|:---:|
| *Anthemis tinctoria* (Dyer's chamomile) | | | ✓ |
| *Artemisia abrotanum* (southernwood) | | | ✓ |
| *Borago officinalis* (borage) | ✓ | | |
| *Calendula officinalis* (pot marigold) | ✓ | ✓ | ✓ |
| *Carthamus tinctorius* (safflower) | | | ✓ |
| *Chamaemelum nobile* (Roman chamomile) | ✓ | ✓ | ✓ |
| *Daucus carota* (carrot) | | ✓ | |
| *Echinacea* species (coneflower) | | ✓ | |
| *Equisetum arvense* (horsetail) | | ✓ | ✓ |
| *Foeniculum vulgare* (fennel) | ✓ | ✓ | ✓ |
| *Fragaria vesca* (strawberry) | | ✓ | ✓ |
| *Galium odoratum* (sweet woodruff) | | | ✓ |
| *Glycyrrhiza glabra* (liquorice) | ✓ | | |
| *Hamamelis virginiana* (witch hazel) | | ✓ | |
| *Hypericum perforatum* (St John's wort) | ✓ | | |
| *Hyssopus officinalis* (hyssop) | ✓ | | |
| *Iris germanica* var. *florentina* (orris) | | | ✓ |

## List of Herbs Mentioned in the Book and Their Uses

| | First-aid | Cosmetic | In the Home |
|---|---|---|---|
| *Isatis tinctoria* (woad) | | | ✓ |
| *Lavandula angustifolia* (lavender) | ✓ | ✓ | ✓ |
| *Matricaria recutita* (German chamomile) | ✓ | ✓ | ✓ |
| *Melissa officinalis* (lemon balm) | | ✓ | |
| *Mentha pulegium* (pennyroyal) | | | ✓ |
| *Mentha spicata* (spearmint) | ✓ | ✓ | ✓ |
| *Mentha* x *piperata* (peppermint) | ✓ | ✓ | ✓ |
| *Ocimum basilicum* (sweet basil) | | | ✓ |
| *Ocimum tenuiflorum* (holy basil) | ✓ | | |
| *Origanum majorana* (sweet marjoram) | | ✓ | |
| *Origanum vulgare* (oregano) | ✓ | ✓ | |
| *Pelargonium capitatum* (rose-scented pelargonium) | ✓ | | ✓ |
| *Petroselinum crispum* (parsley) | ✓ | ✓ | ✓ |
| *Pimpinella anisum* (aniseed) | ✓ | ✓ | ✓ |
| *Plantago major* (plantain) | ✓ | | |
| *Rosa gallica* var. *officinalis* (Apothecary's rose) | ✓ | ✓ | ✓ |
| *Rosmarinus officinalis* (rosemary) | ✓ | ✓ | ✓ |

| | First-aid | Cosmetic | In the Home |
|---|:---:|:---:|:---:|
| *Ruta graveoloens* (rue) | | | ✓ |
| *Salvia officinalis* (sage) | ✓ | ✓ | ✓ |
| *Sambucus nigra* (elder) | ✓ | ✓ | |
| *Saponaria officinalis* (soapwort) | | ✓ | ✓ |
| *Satureja montana* (winter savory) | ✓ | | |
| *Stachys officinalis* (woundwort) | ✓ | | |
| *Symphytum officinale* (comfrey) | ✓ | ✓ | |
| *Tanacetum parthenium* (feverfew) | ✓ | | ✓ |
| *Tanacetum vulgare* (tansy) | | | ✓ |
| *Thymus vulgaris* (thyme) | ✓ | ✓ | |
| *Tropaeolum majus* (nasturtium) | ✓ | ✓ | |
| *Urtica dioica* (nettle) | | ✓ | |
| *Valeriana officinalis* (valerian) | ✓ | | ✓ |
| *Verbascum thrapsus* (mullein) | ✓ | | |
| *Zingiber officinale* (ginger) | ✓ | | |

# *Glossary of Main Terms Used in this Book*

COMPRESS

Compresses can be either cold, hot, or in-between, depending on what you want to use them for. A cold compress will help to reduce swelling and is useful on bruises and sprains. To make a cold compress, simply soak a flannel in an infusion or decoction and apply it to the area. A hot compress, or fomentation, can be useful in reducing muscle tension and improving poor circulation. Again, you soak a flannel in an infusion or decoction, but this time it needs to be as hot as can be borne. A warm compress is useful to ease some headaches.

## Decoction

A decoction is very similar to an infusion (see below). The ratio of herbs to water is the same, but you simmer the herbs in the water for 10 to 15 minutes, rather than just pouring hot water over them. This method is used for tougher or woody material like roots.

## Infusion or Tea or Tisane

An infusion is the most straightforward way of preparing herbs. It is, in effect, a herbal tea and you make it in exactly the same way as ordinary tea, by pouring hot water over the leaves, flowers or stems of the herb and leaving them to steep for about ten minutes. Strain the herbs and there you have it!

The usual ratio of herbs to water is 25g of dried herbs *or* 50g fresh herbs to 600ml of water.

## Oils

The sort of oils I am talking about here are those which are made by the infusion or decoction method, but using oil instead of water.

Essential oils are quite different and are obtained by extracting the oil from plant material by steam distillation: this is best left to specialist, commercial producers.

To make an infused oil simply put a quantity of herb(s) in a clear jar and pour over 250ml of vegetable oil. Pop on the lid and leave the jar in a sunny place for two to three weeks.

Then strain the oil through a fine mesh sieve and pour it into a bottle. Keep the oil in a cool place, but warm it a little before you use it.

An oil decoction can also be made. A double saucepan is ideal for this recipe, but a heat-proof bowl over a pan of simmering water will do just as well.

Put 300g of vegetable oil in the pan or bowl and heat gently until it is liquid. Roughly chop equal quantities of herbs: you will need enough so that they remain submerged in the oil. Leave the oil and herbs over a very low heat for a couple of hours by which time the herbs will have released their beneficial and aromatic properties. Strain the oil through a muslin cloth into sterilised ointment jars (see page 192) and keep them in a cool place.

POULTICE

A poultice also involves applying a cloth to the affected area; this time the herb or mixture of herbs, enclosed in gauze, is applied directly. To be effective the herbs must be moist, so if you use fresh herbs, soften them with a little warm water. Dried herbs should be moistened with hot water too, and made into paste. Put the herbs between two pieces of gauze and apply to the area, keeping the gauze in place with a bandage. The poultice should be kept as warm as possible; the easiest way to do this is to cover it with a hot water bottle.

A poultice is particularly useful if you want to draw toxins from the body. Boils and splinters, in particular, respond well to this treatment.

## STERILISE

Whatever containers you use to keep your herbs or preparations in, you will need to sterilise them before you can use them.

If your containers are heat-proof, you can wash and rinse them thoroughly and then pop them in the oven, heated to a temperature of 100°C, for at least ten minutes. Allow them to cool before you use them.

Another method, for non-heat-proof containers, is to use a proprietary sterilising solution of the kind you sterilise babies' bottles with. To make the solution, simply follow the instructions on the bottle or packet. Make sure the containers are thoroughly drained and dry before you use them.

Don't sterilise any container too far in advance, otherwise the germ-free conditions will be lost.

## TEA

– see Infusion

## TISANE

– see Infusion

# Useful Addresses and Websites

HERB RELATED

Nearly all good garden centres and nurseries sell herb plants and/or seeds.

Here are a few more specialist nurseries should you fail to find what you want locally. Please contact them first to find out if and when they are open to the public before making a special journey – some are just mail order.

As well as these suppliers, the venues listed on the 'Herb Gardens to Visit' page will invariably have herb plants for sale.

*The Garden Studio*
www.thegarden-studio.co.uk
01772 812672
Specialist perennial nursery
– a wide range of herbs are available.
Also short courses on herbs and other subjects.

*Arne Herbs*
www.arneherbs.co.uk
01275 333399

*Downderry Nursery*
www.downderry-nursery.co.uk
01732 810081
Lavender and rosemary specialist

*Hooksgreen Herbs*
www.hooksgreenherbs.com
07977 883810
Herb growers

*Iden Croft Herbs*
www.uk-herbs.com
01580 891432
Herb growers – beautiful garden

*Jekka's Herb Farm*
www.jekkasherbfarm.com
01454 418878
Organic herb specialist with a unique 'herboretum'

*Pepperpot Nursery*
www.pepperpotherbplants.co.uk
01483 424614

*Suffolk Herbs*
www.suffolkherbs.com
01376 572456
Supplier of herb seeds

DYESTUFF SUPPLIER

*Wild Colours*
www.wildcolours.co.uk
07979 770 865

SUPPLIERS OF HERBAL
INGREDIENTS AND
PREPARATIONS

*Neal's Yard Remedies*
www.nealsyardremedies.com
0845 2623145
Also www.uk-nyrorganic/shop/
MaureenLittle

*The Organic Herb Trading
Company*
www.organicherbtrading.com
01823 401205

# *Herb Gardens to Visit*

**P**lease check with the venue before you plan your visit as some may have limited opening times.

All botanical gardens will have herbs of interest, as will all the Royal Horticultural Society's gardens.

Acorn Bank Garden, Penrith, Cumbria: www.nationaltrust.org.uk/ acorn-bank

Chelsea Physic Garden, London: www.chelseaphysicgarden.co.uk

## *Herb Gardens to Visit*

Dilston Physic Garden, Dilston Mill House, near Corbridge, Northumberland: www.dilstonphysicgarden.com

Hardwick Hall, Doe Lea, Chesterfield: www.nationaltrust.org.uk/hardwick

Herb Garden, Hardstoft, Derbyshire: www.theherbgarden.co.uk

Iden Croft Herbs, Staplehurst, Kent: www.uk-herbs.com

Jekka's Herb Farm near Bristol: www.jekkasherbfarm.com

Royal Horticultural Society's Garden, Wisley, Surrey: www.rhs.org

The Herb Society's National Herb Garden, Sulgrave Manor, Banbury: www.sulgravemanor.co.uk

The Queen's Garden, Royal Botanic Gardens Kew: www.kew.org

# Index of Herbs

*Achillea millefolium*
*Allium sativum*
*Aloe vera*
*Aloysia triphylla*
*Althaea officinalis*
*Anethum graveolens*
*Anthemis tinctoria*
*Artemisia abrotanum*

*Borago officinalis*

*Calendula officinalis*
*Carthamus tinctorius*
*Chamaemelum nobile*

*Daucus carota*

*Echinacea* species
*Equisetum arvense*

*Foeniculum vulgare*
*Fragaria vesca*
*Galium odoratum*
*Glycyrrhiza glabra*

*Hamamelis virginiana*
*Hypericum perforatum*
*Hyssopus officinalis*

*Iris germanica* var. *florentina*
*Isatis tinctoria*

*Lavandula angustifolia*

*Matricaria recutita*
*Melissa officinalis*
*Mentha pulegium*
*Mentha spicata*
*Mentha* x *piperata*

*Ocimum basilicum*
*Ocimum tenuiflorum*
*Origanum majorana*
*Origanum vulgare*

*Pelargonium capitatum*
*Petroselinum crispum*
*Pimpinella anisum*
*Plantago major*

*Rheum rhabarbarum*
*Rhus typhina*
*Rosa gallica* var. *officinalis*
*Rosmarinus officinalis*
*Ruta graveoloens*

*Salvia officinalis*
*Sambucus nigra*
*Saponaria officinalis*
*Satureja montana*
*Stachys officinalis*
*Symphytum officinale*

## Index of Herbs

# Index